P. A. Hopkins – July 12. 1923.

Old Cottages
and
Farmhouses
in
Surrey

Old Cottages and Farmhouses in Surrey

Photographed by W. Galsworthy Davie

With an Introduction and Sketches by W. Curtis Green A.R.I.B.A.

London
B. T. Batsford
94, High Holborn

1908

Windham Press is committed to bringing the lost cultural heritage of ages past into the 21st century through high-quality reproductions of original, classic printed works at affordable prices.

This book has been carefully crafted to utilize the original images of antique books rather than error-prone OCR text. This also preserves the work of the original typesetters of these classics, unknown craftsmen who laid out the text, often by hand, of each and every page you will read. Their subtle art involving judgment and interaction with the text is in many ways superior and more human than the mechanical methods utilized today, and gave each book a unique, hand-crafted feel in its text that connected the reader organically to the art of bindery and book-making.

We think these benefits are worth the occasional imperfection resulting from the age of these books at the time of scanning, and their vintage feel provides a connection to the past that goes beyond the mere words of the text.

As bibliophiles, we are always seeking perfection in our work, and so please notify us of any errors in this book by emailing us at corrections@windhampress.com. Our team is motivated to correct errors quickly so future customers are better served. Our mission is to raise the bar of quality for reprinted works by a focus on detail and quality over mass production.

To peruse our catalog of carefully curated classic works, please visit our online store at www.windhampress.com.

PREFACE

I AM asked by Mr. Davie and by Mr. Batsford to preface my introduction with an expression of their thanks to the owners or occupiers of cottages or houses who have helped in the making of this book. Every photographer will appreciate the difficulties which have had to be contended with; a good photograph would often have been impossible without the kind offices of those living in the houses. In my own less arduous task the kindnesses I experienced never failed to impress the charm of the buildings more strongly on my mind. A preface gives me the opportunity of recording my respectful admiration for the patience and tenacity with which Mr. Davie—now no longer an active member of the architectural profession—has carried through his undertaking. The present collection of illustrations is one of a series, the previous volumes of which have treated of similar work in other counties. The series originated in Mr. Davie's beautiful photographs, and it is to these that the publication of this volume is due.

The subject of "The old cottage and domestic architecture of South-west Surrey" is the title of a work by Mr. Ralph Nevill, a work well known among architects and those interested in domestic architecture. Mr. Nevill collected and preserved records, the value of which is generally recognized. His book was a mine of information to me before this volume was ever contemplated, and it is in no emulative spirit that I have undertaken a further contribution on the subject. The lapse of seventeen years since the last edition of Mr. Nevill's book, and the scope of the subject itself, would be justification, were one needed, for the publication of the collotype plates from these photographs.

Mr. Davie's experience in the other volumes of this series no doubt made my part lighter than it would otherwise have been. He found several of the buildings illustrated, and drew my attention to some of their details.

Amongst others, my thanks are due to the Rev. Gerald S. Davies, of Godalming, and to Mr. Penfold, of Haslemere, for pointing out interesting examples. Mr. Penfold also kindly lent some of his photographic views, shown in the text, of cottages since disfigured by the hand of the restorer. Mr. George Jack and Mr. A. B. Hayward have supplied me with valuable matter regarding Great Tangley and the Guest House at Lingfield respectively. My brother, Mr. A. Romney Green, of Haslemere, has helped me throughout with criticism and counsel. My notes make no claim to originality of thought or research; the authority for statements of facts are the recognized text-books upon English domestic architecture, and are, as far as I am aware, duly acknowledged in the footnotes.

W. CURTIS GREEN.

14, GRAY'S INN SQUARE,
  LONDON, W.C.
    April, 1908.

ALPHABETICAL LIST OF PLATES

ARRANGED UNDER NAMES OF TOWNS AND VILLAGES

	Plate
ABINGER (NEAR), CROSSWAYS FARM	18, 19
,, ,, WOLVENS FARM	100
ALFOLD, COTTAGE AT	1
,, COTTAGES BY THE CHURCH	2, 3
ASH, IN THE VILLAGE	3
,, MANOR FARM	4
,, THE VILLAGE STREET	5
BEDDINGTON, COTTAGES, CHURCH GREEN	6, 7
BLETCHINGLY, FARM-HOUSE, BREWER STREET	8
,, COTTAGES NEAR THE CHURCH	9
BRIMSCOMBE, CHIMNEY AND ENTRANCE AT	11
,, COTTAGE AT	10
CHIDDINGFOLD, COMBE FARM	13
,, COTTAGE AT	15
,, (NEAR) WEST END FARM	12
,, THE CROWN INN	16
,, THE OLD VICARAGE	14
COMPTON, A COTTAGE AT	17
CROWHURST PLACE, VIEW ACROSS THE MOAT	20
,, WARREN FARM-HOUSE	21

LIST OF PLATES

	Plate
EASHING, Cottages at	22, 23
,, Cottages by the River	24
,, (near)	29
ELSTEAD, Cottages at	16, 89
EWHURST, Cottages at	28, 29
,, Northlands Farm	25, 26
,, Pollingfold Farm-house, Ellens Green	27
,, Summersbury Farm-house	30
FARNCOMBE, Cottages at	33
,, The Almshouses	31, 32
FARNHAM, Castle Street	34
,, Downing Street	36
,, (near) Farm-house and Footbridge	35
,, Oriel Window	35
,, View up Fir Grove	36
FRENSHAM, Cottage at	37
,, Spreakley Farm-house	38
FROSBURY Farm-house	39
,, and Littlefield, Farms between	40
GODALMING (near), Unstead Farm-house	41, 42
,, ,, Hurtmore Farm-house	81
GODSTONE, Church Road	43
GOMSHALL, Houses at	44, 90
GUILDFORD (near), Compton's Farm, Wood Street	45
,, ,, Cottages	46
,, ,, Manor Farm, East Shalford	60
HAMBLEDON, Cottages at	32, 56

LIST OF PLATES

	Plate
HASLEMERE, Cottages at	48, 49
,, Shepherd's Hill	47
HORLEY (near), Smallfield Place	82
LINGFIELD, Cottages at	52
,, Shop and Cottage	51
,, The Guest House (W Page, Photo.)	50
LITTLEFIELD Farm-house	98
MAYFORD, Woking, Cottage at	92
MILFORD, at Moushill	53
,, (near) Cottage at Nine Elms	55
,, Farm-houses at	54
,, Tiled Cottage	56
NEWDIGATE, Cottages at Kingsland	59
,, (near), the "Surrey Oaks" Inn	60
NORMANDY VILLAGE (near), Farm-house and Cottages	58
,, ,, ,, Ruined Cottage; Cottages	57
OCKLEY (near), Bonnet's Farm	61, 62
,, ,, Oscroft's or Street's Farm	63
OXTED (near), Stockhurst Farm	33
,, ,, Back of "Stud House"	46
RIPLEY Cottages at	66
,, Hole, Cottage	67
,, The "Anchor" Inn	65
SEALE, East End Farm-house	68, 69, 70
SHAMLEY GREEN, The Post Office	71, 72, 73

LIST OF PLATES

	Plate
SHAMLEY GREEN, Cottage at	74, 76
,, ,, Detail View of Gable	75
SHERE, Cottages at	55, 77, 78
SLYFIELD GREEN (near Guildford), Cottages at	80, 81
,, ,, Woodlands Farm	79
STOKE (near Guildford), Cottages at	83, 84
,, ,, ,, Slyfield Farm	97
TANGLEY MANOR, GREAT	85, 86
THURSLEY, Cottages at	89, 90
,, Cottage near the Inn	88
,, (near) Cottage	87
TONGHAM, Barn at	91
,, Cartshed and Granary	91
,, and Farnham, Cottages between	5, 92
WITLEY, Cottages near the Church at	96
,, The Manor Farm	97
,, The Village Street	95
,, The "White Hart" Inn	94
,, (near) A Gabled Farm-house	76
,, ,, Tigbourne Farm	93
WORPLESDEN, Cottage in Village	58
,, Hurst Cottages	98
,, Norton Farm-house	99

INDEX TO ILLUSTRATIONS IN TEXT

Fig. Number		Page
	Abbot's Hospital, Guildford, *v.* under Guildford.	
72.	Alfold, Chimney	55
99.	„ Glazing	67
55.	Ash Manor Farm-house, Staircase	41
70.	„ „ „ Chimney	54
25, 26.	Barge boards	23
95.	Bed wagon	65
6.	Beddington, The Old Post Office	6
20.	Bletchingly, A Gable	21
92.	„ Hour Glass Stand	65
36.	Bramley, A Cottage	32
34.	Brewer Street Farm, Detail of Angle Post	30
35, 49.	„ „ „ Doorway	31, 38
43.	„ „ „ Wooden Mouldings	34
2.	Brooke, Cottages at	3
	(J. W. Penfold, photo.)	
84.	Casement Fastener	61
42.	Chiddingfold, The *Crown Inn*	34
68, 69, 70, 71, 72.	Chimney Stacks	53, 54, 55
67.	Chimney, Typical Forms of	52
96.	Crowhurst Place, Wooden Candelabrum	66
38.	„ „ Floor	32
65, 66.	„ „ Interiors	50, 51
	(From C. Baily, *Remarks on Timber Houses*)	
82.	„ „ Knocker	61
41.	„ „ Oak Panelling	33
43.	„ „ Wooden Mouldings	34
35, 50, 51, 52, 77.	Doors	31, 39, 40, 59
24.	Dormer Window, A	22
102.	Eashing, A Well at	68
	(W. Galsworthy Davie, photo.)	
3.	East Horsley, Cottage at	3
	(J. W. Penfold, photo.)	

INDEX TO ILLUSTRATIONS IN TEXT

Fig. Number				Page
7.	East Shalford, Manor Farm			7
	(W. Galsworthy Davie, photo.)			
28, 30.	Ewhurst, Weather Tiling			25, 26
78.	Farncombe, Almshouses at			60
	(W. Galsworthy Davie, photo.)			
75.	Farnham, Cottage at			58
90.	,, Entrance Gateway			63
	(W. Galsworthy Davie, photo.)			
43.	,, Fir Grove Hill, Wooden Mouldings			34
25, 26.	,, Barge Board in Oak			23
91	,, Ironwork of Gateway			64
45.	,, Mouldings in			36
93.	,, A Vane			65
15.	Frensham, A Gamekeeper's Cottage			16
86.	Footscraper			61
20, 24, 27, 61.	Gables			21, 22, 24, 45
16, 98, 99, 100.	Glazing			17, 67
73, 74.	Godalming, Ornamental Brickwork			56, 57
	(W. Galsworthy Davie, photo.)			
63.	Godstone, A Fireplace			48
40.	,, House at			33
19	,, Roof Truss			20
37, 44.	Great Tangley Manor, Detail of Window at			32, 35
	(W. Galsworthy Davie, photo.)			
77.	,, ,, ,, Doorway at			59
9.	,, ,, ,, Plan of House and Gardens			11
17.	,, ,, ,, Roof Truss			18
97	Guildford, Abbot's Hospital, Candelabrum at			66
52.	,, ,, ,, Door at			40
103.	,, ,, ,, Lead Rainwater Heads			69
58.	,, ,, ,, Fireside Settle at			43
57.	,, ,, ,, Table and Bench at			42
48.	,, Bay Window			38

INDEX TO ILLUSTRATIONS IN TEXT

Fig. Number		Page
31.	Guildford, Cottage in Farnham Road	27
46, 47.	,, High Street, Bay Windows at	37
101, 103.	,, Lead Rainwater Heads at	67, 69
28.	Hascombe, Weather Tiling at	25
8.	Haslemere, Cottage at	10
	(W. Galsworthy Davie, photo.)	
14.	,, Near	15
	(J. W. Penfold, photo.)	
27.	,, Gables in the High Street	24
28.	,, Weather Tiling at	25
79, 80.	Hinge, Iron and Ornamental	60
82, 83, 84, 85, 86, 89, 91, 93, 94.	Ironwork	61, 62, 64, 65
81, 83.	Knockers	61
5.	Leigh Hill, Cobham, Cottages at	5
	(Frith & Co., Reigate, photo.)	
18.	Lingfield, The Guest House, Details of the Hall	19
10.	,, ,, ,, ,, Plans of the	12
33.	,, Shop at	29
85.	Lock and Bolt	61
100.	Milford, Glazing at	67
40, 43, 45.	Moulding	33, 34, 36
50.	Newdigate, Doorway at	39
68.	Ockley, Bonnet's Farm, Chimney at	53
54.	,, ,, ,, Newel at	41
56.	,, ,, ,, Oak Trestle Table and Benches at	42
98.	Oxted, Glazing at	67
39, 41, 44.	Panelling	33, 35
94.	Pipe Rack	65
9, 10, 15.	Plans of Cottages	11, 12, 16
60.	Platters, Old Wooden	44
	(H. D. Gower, photo.)	

INDEX TO ILLUSTRATIONS IN TEXT

Fig. Number		Page
28.	Prestwick, Weather Tiling	25
51.	Puttenden, A Doorway	39
64.	Racks, Spit	49
71.	Rake House, Chimney	54
39.	Rede Place, Beam and Panelling	33
32.	Ripley, Newark Mill, near	28
	(Frith & Co., Reigate, photo.)	
11, 12, 13, 17, 19.	Roof Construction	14, 18, 20
88.	Rushlight Holder	61
87.	Scold's Bridle	61
76.	Seale, Window in Farmhouse at	58
56, 57, 58.	Seats, Benches, etc	42, 43
15, 18, 21.	Sections of Cottages, etc.	16, 19, 21
29.	Shalford, Weather Tiling at	26
69.	Shottermill, Chimney	53
64.	Spit Racks	49
59.	Stoke D'Abernon, Church Chest at	43
	(G. C. Druce, photo.)	
16.	Summersbury Farmhouse, Ewhurst	17
1.	Sutton, near Abinger, Cottages at	1
	(W. Galsworthy Davie, photo.)	
28, 29.	Tiling	25, 26
23.	Tongham, Cottage at	22
46, 47, 48, 76.	Windows	37, 38, 58
22.	Wipley Farmyard	21
	(W. Galsworthy Davie, photo.)	
21.	„ Farm, Section of a Barn	21
28.	Witley, Weather Tiling at	25
61.	Woking Village, Brick Gables in	45
53.	Wolvens Farm, Back Entrance	40
4.	Woodgate Green, Epsom, Cottages at	4
	(Frith & Co., Reigate, photo.)	

FIG. I. A SURREY HAMLET, SUTTON, NEAR ABINGER.

Old Cottages and Farm-houses in Surrey

THESE cottages and farm-houses are the work of generations of unknown English craftsmen rather than of famous or clever individuals. The interest attaching to them is more nearly that of a living tradition than of an historical style. They have a breath of life about them for us to-day which is significant to an increasing number. There is, too, more general regret than was once the case at the destruction of old buildings, joined in even by those who do not appreciate their full worth. The efforts to preserve old work are better organized, and show an increasing sense of responsibility towards that which remains unspoiled. Where preservation is impossible it is becoming a recognized duty to record as faithfully as possible the characteristics of the old work. For this purpose I think there is no doubt that photographs are superior to sketches, though photographs alone are not an ideal record; accompanied with figured diagrams they are perhaps the best that can be done until organized surveys of the old houses in this country are collected. There are probably many careful scale plans and sectional drawings made by responsible students in existence; these would be invaluable supplemented with photographs, and housed where they would be accessible, as for instance with the Phené Spiers Collection at the Victoria and Albert Museum. The making of such surveys is the best introduction to domestic architecture that the student can have. To omit measuring and drawing on the spot is to know little of the simplicity of structure, the laborious handwork, and the fancy arising from it, which ennobles old work. Draughtsmanship has well defined limits of usefulness, and in no other school are these so readily learnt, for here is the baffling factor apparent in every work of art, which it is impossible to convey to paper in terms of measurement. Some of these old buildings are works of art, that is, they show that intangible quality, the result of growth and life, which no artificial rules or mechanical means can achieve; those employed on the building were doing creative work, according to their capacity for their fellows, who were competent to appreciate success or failure.

The destruction of ancient houses with their associations is a serious enough matter in any country, even after it has well con-

FIG. 2. AT BROOKE—BEFORE ALTERATION, TAKEN IN 1885.

FIG. 3. COTTAGES AT EAST HORSLEY.

sidered with what to replace them. To us, such houses as these illustrated by Mr. Davie, essentially English in design and workmanship, are a heritage; they are gradually disappearing, and being replaced with our own work. If it were not that an increasing number of our new houses are built on principles comparable to those exemplified by the best old work, the position would be deplorable indeed. To some, unfortunately to some

FIG. 4. WOODGATE GREEN, EPSOM.

of the most cultured, it is without hope. Yet, if we consider the degraded state to which the art of building sank during the earlier half of the last century, we shall appreciate the improvement that is taking place. The rise of new conditions and new ideals in society happily does not imply the total loss of what was best in earlier times, though first principles may be lost sight of in the passing experiments of the untrained. Our connection with these old houses is really no distant one, it has only been broken off; in getting into touch with them again we need not be archaeologists and antiquarians, but makers of things for present use, learning principles of fitness and construction and methods of workmanship that will bring out the best qualities of the workman and the material. We need a traditional building art, that will enrich life, and add to the pleasure of the country side.

The small houses of the country towns and villages, and the cottages on the common (Plates xxxiv, xxxvi, Figs. 1–5) are more than historical relics; the forms which they take are dictated by principles which can never be old or out of date. In building of a utili-

FIG. 5. LEIGH HILL, COBHAM.

tarian character, such as cottages and small houses, economy is necessarily one of the dominating factors. When Emerson said " that the line of beauty was the line of perfect economy," he was only putting into words what has so often been shown in building. Architecture is no exotic aloof from the facts of life; it has to express the needs and ideals of the time, and cannot thrive apart from them.

It is obvious to the most superficial that economics act directly upon building and the allied arts. Architecture has always been a transcript of history, showing the defects and virtues in the life of those producing it. Thus the central fact in considering the continuous history of domestic architecture is the break in the continuity of its development which began, during the last part of the eighteenth century, with the introduction of the factory system and the rapid development of machinery. The machine took the place of the craftsman, and set up a false standard amongst

FIG. 6. THE OLD POST OFFICE, BEDDINGTON (BEFORE RESTORATION).

employers and employed. Not only did it become master, but it tried to conceal poverty, making it hideous where before it had been homely and unpretending. The quality of traditional work disappeared under these new influences; the old buildings of the cottage class became mere picturesque features in the landscape, devoid of meaning for builders in the nineteenth century. Then came the reaction from the result of these conditions, and an attempt was made to revive the past styles of building, but the tradition had been broken, the requirements were different, and the revival was an imitation only of outward forms which had originally been the outcome of the natural circumstances of

FIG. 7. A SURREY FARMSTEAD—MANOR FARM, EAST SHALFORD.

building. Had it not been for that now famous inner circle of the Gothic revivalists, supported by the writings of Morris and Ruskin, who realized that it was the spirit of the old work which was lacking, the revival would have ended in the imitative school. To them we owe the life and vigour which has marked the best work of recent years. They gathered the broken threads of the old traditions and drew the crafts together. They insisted upon the value of the old work, and the necessity for studying it as the foundation of architectural education and good taste. They showed that it was necessary, in order to form an intelligent opinion upon architecture—other than mere likes and dislikes—to understand the reasonableness and continuity of the various steps which produced architecture in the past. They showed that, important as the systematic study of archaeology is, it is not architecture, but that as a practical standard, as a revival of form rather than of spirit, it is an attractive By-path Meadow leading to Doubting Castle and Giant Despair.

If domestic architecture, therefore, is to be a living subject for us, there is no way but to follow those who have bridged the gap, and brought us in touch with the work of our ancestors, to whom building was an art comprising all the handicrafts and trades. These old buildings are not all beautiful or well built; time has softened many of their faults, and made them almost loveable. Yet through them all runs the same surprising simplicity and bigness in design, the same straightforward methods in solving problems of construction; it is not only the simplicity of the nursery, but the logical and " final refuge of the complex."

The character of the country districts, and the state of society in the Middle Ages, is described in the ninth chapter of the third volume of Hallam's *Middle Ages*. The country presented great tracts of forest lands, the timber from which played so large a part in building. Grant Allen, writing on some of the farm-houses of Surrey in the *English Illustrated Magazine* some years ago, explains the local significance of the names of some of the villages, and the way in which the wilder parts came under cultivation. The early pioneers were the swineherd and the woodman; the first found food for his herd in the acorns of the vast oak forests, which were called *dens;* the second, following, made the clearings, called *fields*, or felled spaces. As these came under cultivation, parts were fenced off by the shepherds for *folds*. All these words are found as terminals in the names of the villages of Surrey and the Weald. Lullenden, Deepdene, Puttenden, Limpsfield, Lingfield, Chiddingfold, and Alfold, are villages with names of local significance. Again, the *leys* are the cleared lands, and the *hursts* the densely wooded ones; such for instance are Tuesley, Bramley, Crowhurst and Ewhurst. Other names show the woodland character of Surrey: Oakwood, Holmwood—holm being the old English name for holly—Farnham, Lingfield, Cranleigh, Elmhurst, and the rest.

The coombes in the deep-wooded bottoms, and near the fords of the streams, were the building sites of our ancestors, who dwelt low on the rich soils of the valleys rather than on the heights as we do to-day.

The charm of the county is not due to geological formation alone, though it has unusual variety of scenery, and extraordinary seclusion in its inner recesses; it is in part due to economic development. Surrey was in the sixteenth and seventeenth centuries a centre of manufacture and trade. The Weald of Surrey, Kent and Sussex was the birthplace of the Iron Trade. The flourishing condition of this trade, and other industries which throve concurrently with it in Tudor days, gave us many country houses, and villages then enjoyed great prosperity for a time, until the coalfields of the north usurped the place of the forests in the south. The removal of the iron industries at an early stage in their development, left relics of building and the crafts that in all probability would have otherwise been swept away. These latter are of particular interest to the many people who are trying to establish conditions in which the workman may again make the necessities of life in building and the lesser arts with proper materials, so put together that they satisfy the eye, and instil a wholesome pride and pleasure into the life of the worker.

The characteristics of Surrey building are not very different from those of Kent and Sussex. Our ancestors used the local materials in whatever county they were building; and they thus produced a tradition of use and design in their work in keeping with the country-side. Some districts, such as the Cotswolds and parts of Yorkshire, and Westmorland, are dependent on one local building material; in these the houses are stone-built and stone-roofed, and are entirely satisfying. In Surrey the local materials are more numerous. East End Farm, Seale (Plates LXVIII, LXIX), shows walls of stone and brick, half timber and plaster, half timber and tile hanging, with a tiled roof. Bonnet's Farm (Plate LXI) has half timbered walls, the panels filled with red brick and lath and plaster, the whole roofed with stone slates. Crowhurst Place (Plate XX) exhibits the building materials of every period, save perhaps its roof covering, which is of stone slates and red tiles, no doubt replacing earlier thatch or wooden shingles. The half-timber house at Ewhurst (Plate XXVIII) still has its stone slated roof, while the stone-built cottage at Haslemere (Fig. 8) is now roofed with red tiles.

FIG. 8. A STONE-BUILT COTTAGE AT HASLEMERE.

All have undergone alterations and additions at the hands of successive generations, but so cunningly done in the traditional way and with such kindly materials that the whole has mellowed together. Some of Mr. Davie's detailed views (notably Plates XXV, XXVI and LXX) give some idea of the colour and texture of these hand-worked, and, in the case of brick and tile, hand-made materials. These are qualities which no machine-made substitute can ever attain.

The nature of the building materials, and the hand labour, are not the only qualities of the old work. The picturesque confusion, where it exists, is the result of successive additions rather

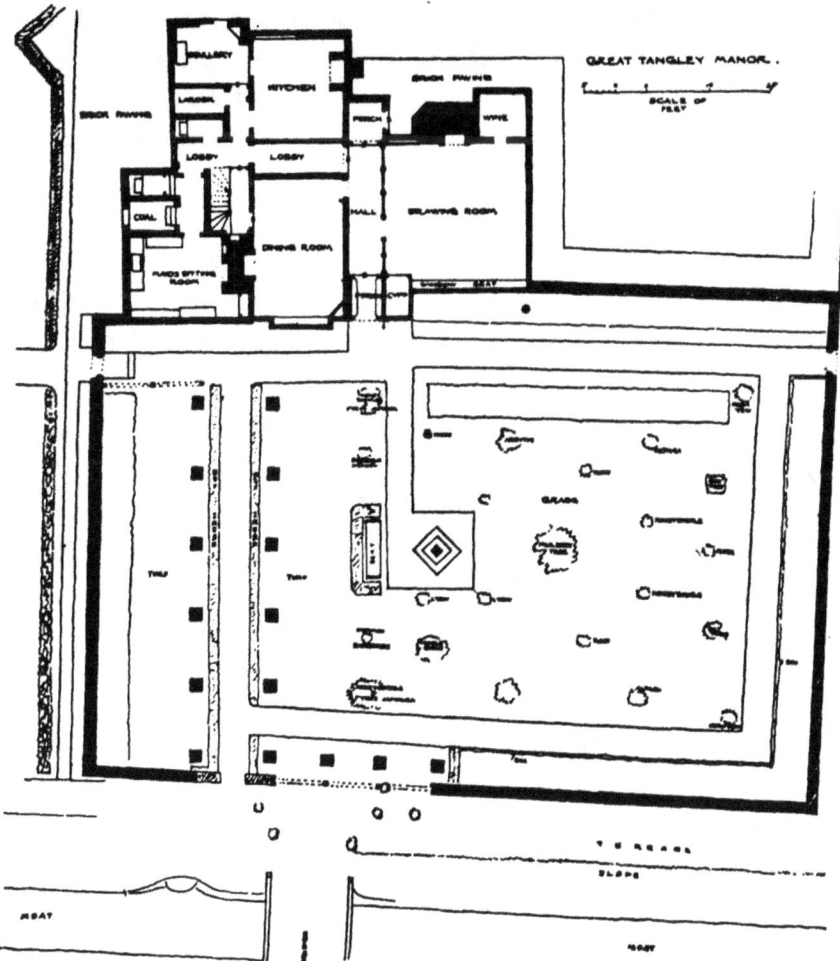

FIG. 9. PLAN OF HOUSE AND GARDENS, GREAT TANGLEY MANOR.

than of conscious effort. The jumble of roofs and gables, the irregular lines of the plans, and the variety of the building materials used, are the accidents of time rather than the attributes of good work. They conceal the underlying simplicity and directness of the original plan, without which no building can be seriously considered as a contribution to architecture.

This is not the place to consider in detail the planning of the larger houses, a few views of which, such as Great Tangley Manor (Plates LXXXV and LXXXVI), are, for special reasons, included in the illustrations. I am indebted to Mr. George Jack for allowing me to make tracings of the ground plan (Fig. 9) and details of the roof from his notes on Great Tangley. This Manor House in its present state is an instance of what can be done to preserve an old house, at the same time adding to its size and convenience. The plan shows Mr. Philip Webb's additions, but not those more recently done by Mr. Jack. The drawing-room was originally the hall, the portion cut from it now marked "hall" is a feature of the mediaeval plan; one side of the hall was usually cut off for a passage by a screen, at one end of which was the principal, at the other the back entrance, the arrangement still obtaining at Great Tangley. The hall was open to the roof, and there was probably a gallery over the screen. The division

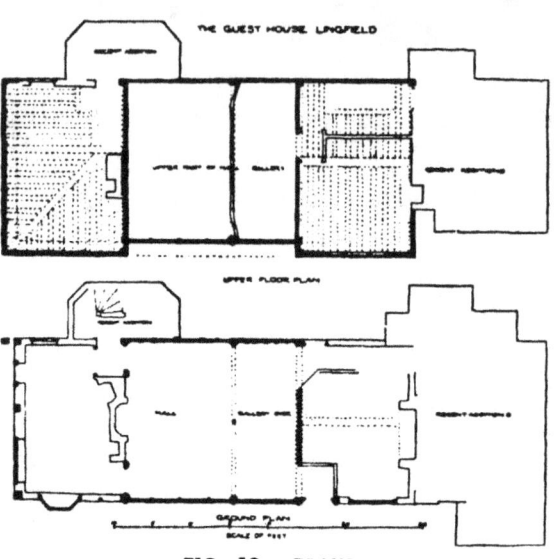

FIG. 10. PLANS.

of the hall into two floors took place probably at the end of the sixteenth century, the date of the present front. The roof truss is part of the early building, and is shown on Fig. 17, p. 18.

By the kindness of Mr. Arthur B. Hayward I am able to give a ground and first-floor plan of the guest house at Lingfield (Fig. 10 and Plate L). When Mr. Hayward's father bought the house, it had unfortunately been divided up, and for some time occupied, as three labourers' cottages; all this was altered, and great care was taken by the late Mr. Hayward to re-establish as much as possible of it in its original state. It is an interesting example of the mediaeval type of plan, with the central hall two stories high, and the offices and bedrooms at either end under the same roof. The chimneys are additions, the fire originally burning in the centre of the room, the smoke escaping through louvres in the roof, a primitive arrangement of that time still found in many yeomen's houses of the sixteenth century. Fig. 18 (p. 19), drawn from materials left by Mr. Hayward, shows some details of the construction of the hall.

The development of the plan of these houses, and details regarding the life of the landowners and their dependants, can be read in Hallam, Turner, Parker, and an exhaustive little book entitled *The Evolution of the English House*, by S. O. Addy, M.Sc., which I shall shortly have reason to quote. The labourers of mediaeval times lived beneath the roofs of their masters' houses and of the monasteries, and no doubt in cottages too of a poor character, but of these no traces remain. With the Reformation, changes took place in the ownership of the land, in the manner of life, and in the housing of the peasant and labouring classes. In the purely agricultural districts the poverty of the people prevented any permanent class of building; it is in flourishing centres of industry like that of Surrey that well-built cottages are found. In these simple buildings of the Tudor and Stuart period we find the traditions of building which in towns and large houses had been abandoned, or modified, by the inroads of foreign workmen and classic ideals. The Renaissance swept the country of Gothic art in high places, but it left the humble phases of building, and the country places of the sixteenth and seventeenth centuries show work very little influenced by the new methods. We thus get a glimpse into times earlier than those actually represented by the dates of the buildings.

It will, I think, be found that the roof construction governed

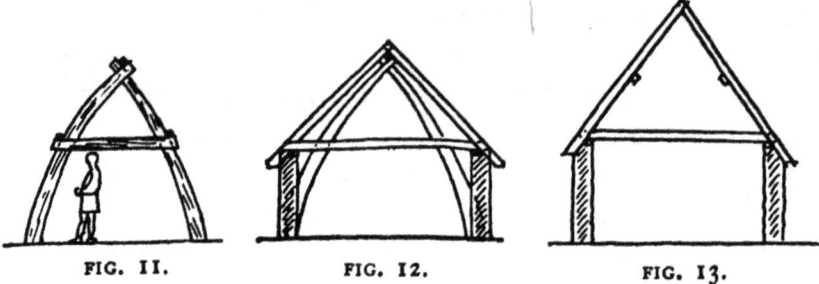

FIG. 11.   FIG. 12.   FIG. 13.

the planning of these cottages, just as, in a greater degree, it governed the plan of a vaulted basilica or a Gothic cathedral. This is indirectly borne out by antiquaries and others who have studied the evolution of house building; they show that the earliest houses were without walls, the roof springing from the ground; the house consisted of a number of roof trusses shaped like the letter A (Fig. 11), spaced about 16 ft. apart,[1] the legs of the A

[1] "In the tenth century English buildings were measured by the linear perch of 16 ft., now 16 ft. 6 in. If we ask ourselves how it was that the perch became the unit we shall see that it was so because 16 feet was the standing room required for four oxen in the stall, and also for the standing room for four oxen in the field, inasmuch as they ploughed abreast. Accordingly the length of the bay, viz. 16 feet, corresponds to the breadth of a rod or rood of land, the acre being composed

—the principal rafters—curved outwards in order that the sides of the house should be as nearly vertical as the construction would allow; the collar of the truss, that is the cross line of the letter A, was sufficiently high to allow of head room for moving about the house. The truss still retained this shape when vertical walls were first added (Fig. 12); the only alteration was that the collar beams were lengthened to rest upon the top of the wall upon a wall plate, the roof itself was then formed of rafters spiked to the ridge piece, supported by the

FIG. 14. NEAR HASLEMERE.

apex of the trusses 16 ft. apart, and to the wooden plate on the top of the low walls. The extension of the length of the house was merely a matter of adding more trusses. Greater width came only with greater skill by forming offshoots at the side or sides.[1] These early forms are worth bearing in mind, they are "the lines of economy," and underlie all subsequent developments.

It was but a step to stand the roof itself upon the wall, and so arrive at the primitive two-roomed cottage, Fig. 13, the upper room in the roof gained by a ladder. This was easily enlarged by

of four roods, each 16 feet broad and 640 feet long, lying side by side. This was the origin of the long as well as of the normal width of a rod of land."—*The Evolution of the English House*, by S. O. Addy, M.Sc.

[1] Addy.

16 OLD COTTAGES AND FARM-HOUSES

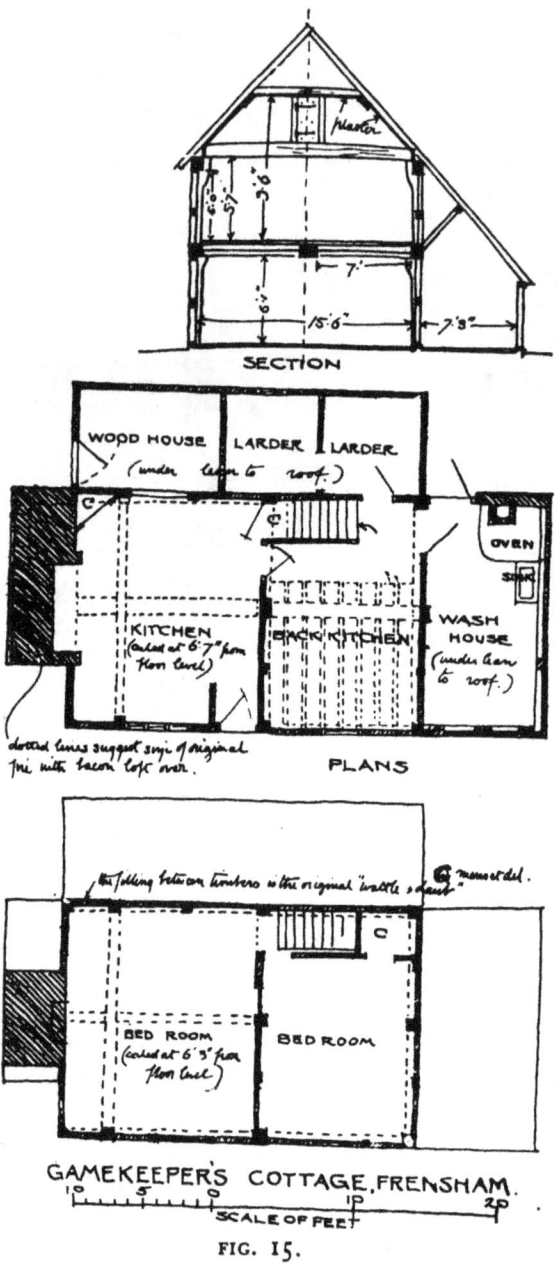

FIG. 15. GAMEKEEPER'S COTTAGE, FRENSHAM.

the addition of another bay to its length, and by carrying down the roof at one side or at the ends, till it nearly touched the ground, as in Figs. 14, 15 and 16, a most economical and incidentally picturesque addition, locally known as a "skilling." The gamekeeper's cottage (Fig. 15) at Frensham shows this last development of plan. It is a typical example of a Surrey cottage, and at present is little spoiled. A good example of the yeoman's house is that of Summersbury Farm (Fig. 16). I am indebted for the illustration to a drawing by Mr. Shuffrey

IN SURREY

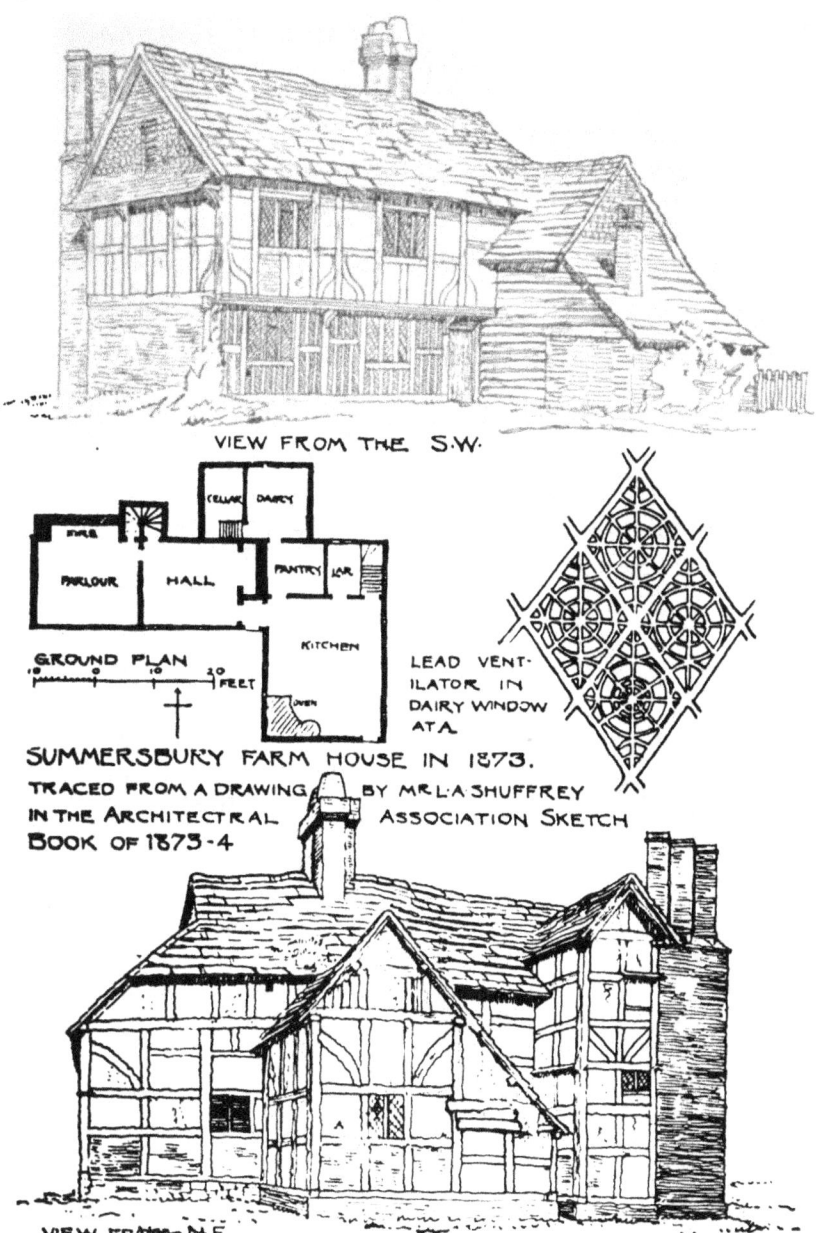

VIEW FROM THE S.W.

LEAD VENTILATOR IN DAIRY WINDOW AT A

SUMMERSBURY FARM HOUSE IN 1873.
TRACED FROM A DRAWING BY MR L.A. SHUFFREY IN THE ARCHITECTRAL ASSOCIATION SKETCH BOOK OF 1873-4

VIEW FROM N.E.

FIG. 16.

18 OLD COTTAGES AND FARM-HOUSES

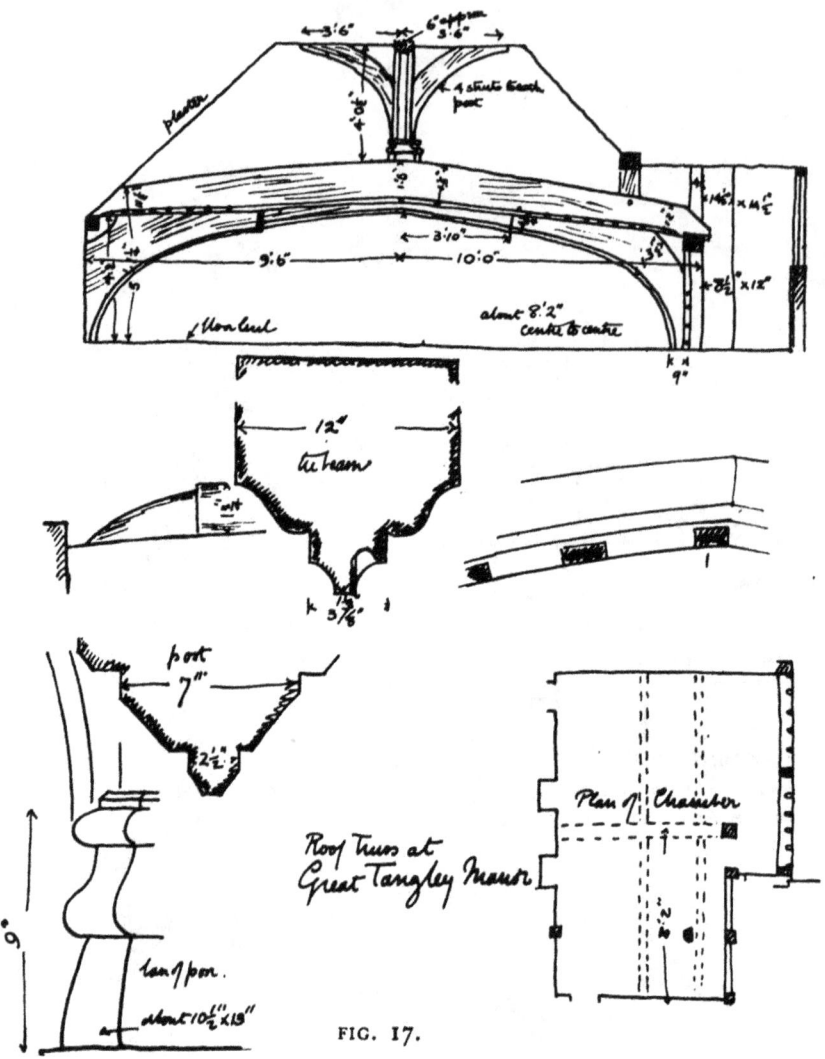

FIG. 17.

which I have traced from the *Architectural Association Sketch Book of* 1873-4. This shows the building before it was re-roofed and otherwise restored (Plate xxx).

The buildings have not the rich open timber roofs, such as make many old mansions famous, but the principles in some of

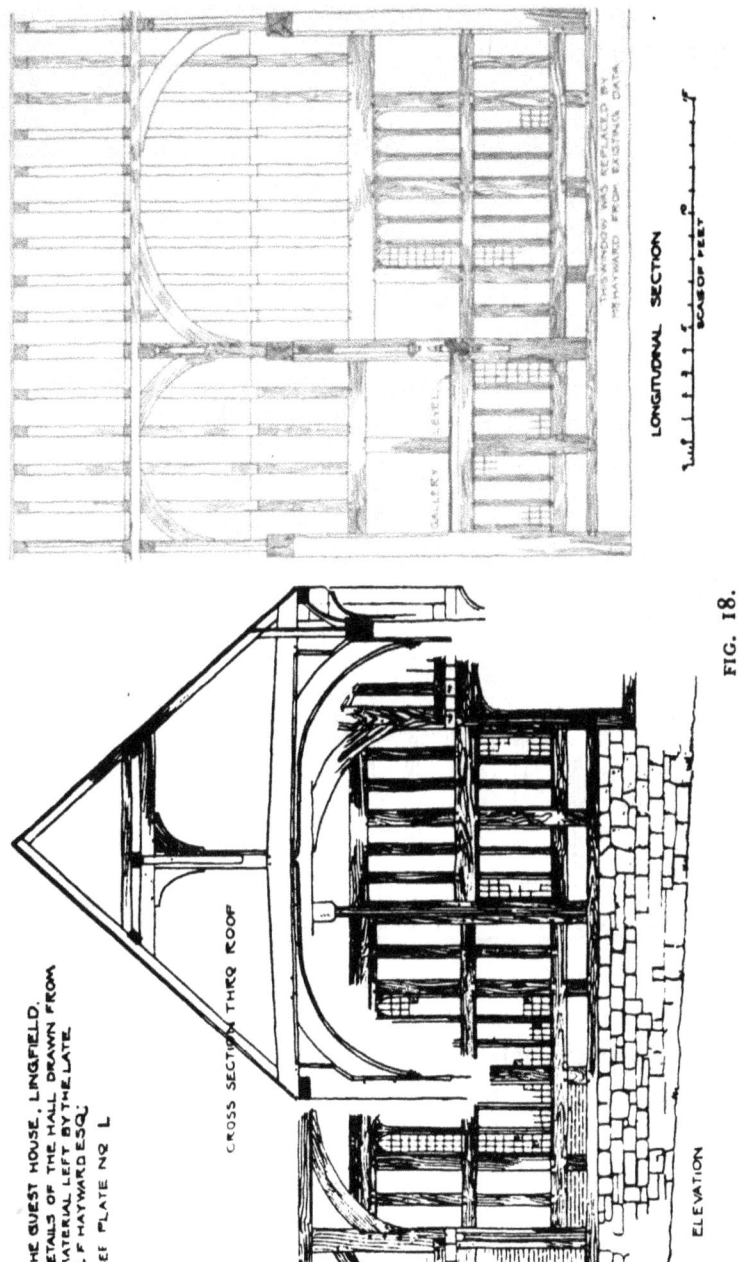

FIG. 18.

the better-class houses are the same, carried out in a rougher and more homely manner.

Fig. 17 shows the roof construction at Great Tangley; Fig. 18 that at the guest house, Lingfield; Fig. 19 a truss to the house at

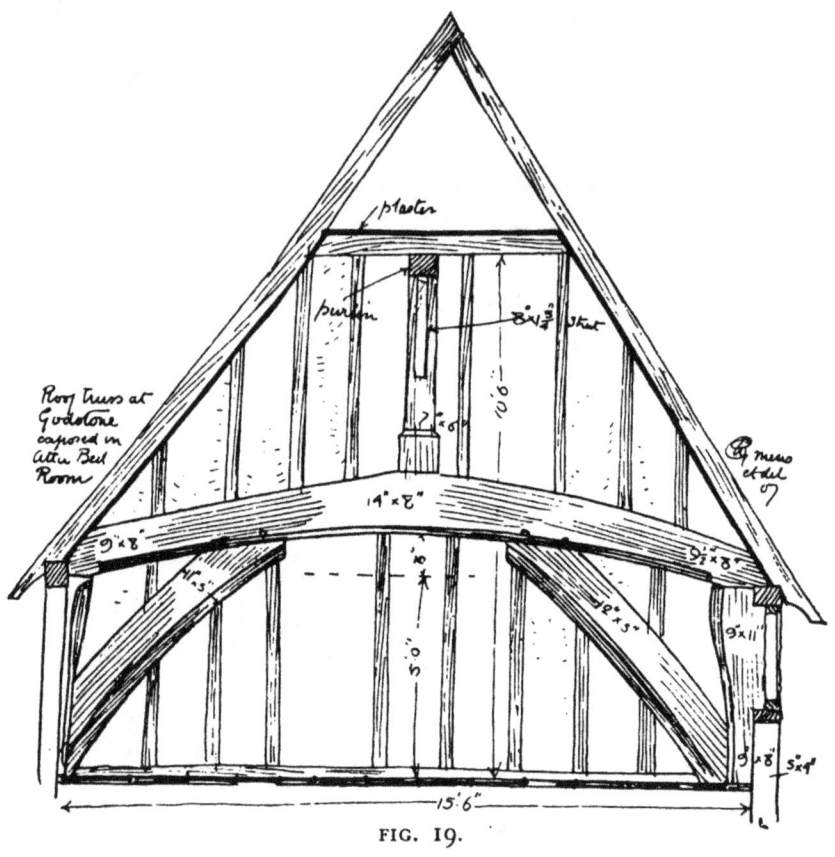

FIG. 19.

Godstone shown on Plate XLIII. In these a collar beam construction is observed, the collars supported by a purlin which is strutted up from the summer beams holding the wall plates. The gable at Bletchingly illustrates the same kind of construction, exposed to view on the outer gable, forming a pleasant piece of design

IN SURREY

(Fig. 20). The roofs of the old barns are instructive, and are probably very nearly allied to the coverings of the mediaeval

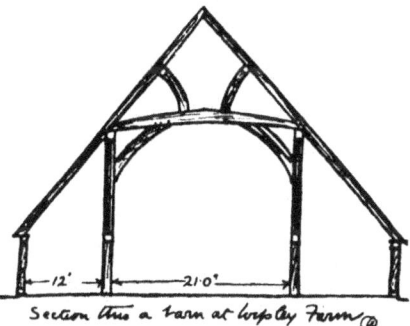

FIG. 20. GABLE AT BLETCHINGLY.

FIG. 21.

FIG. 22. WIPLEY FARMYARD, NEAR NORMANDY.

hall (Figs. 21, 22). The cottages generally show a simple collar beam construction without a truss, though I speak with diffidence, for after getting upstairs the plaster ceiling often defies investigation of the construction above. The collar beam roofs generally show purlins, which rest on the transverse walls of the house, or are supported by the hips of the roof (Fig. 3). The older houses have no gables, the roofs are hipped back where these would come, the eaves of these hips being at a higher level than the main roof, either that the end walls may support the purlins, or that windows may be inserted in the wall to light the rooms in the roof (Fig. 23).

FIG. 23.

FIG. 24.

The earliest roofs are very steeply pitched, and the unbroken surface is one of the charms of the old work; gables and dormer windows as at the *White Hart* at Witley (Plate XCIV) are probably later additions. The *Anchor Inn* at Ripley (Plate LXV) shows the treatment of dormer windows carried further to great perfection. A typical dormer window is shown in Fig. 24. Its last development is shown in the row of shops in the High Street, Haslemere (Fig. 27), where the dormers have developed into a number of gables along the front with only valleys between running back into the main roof. The same treatment often occurs at one end of the building only, as at Plate XLVII, with happy effect. Shamley Green

Post Office (Plate LXXIII) shows this gable very cleverly kept out from the main roof. It was natural to carry the verges of the roof well out over the gable walls; the rafters to support this projection and cover the wall plates and purlins, to which they were housed, were made deep and thin, and with a true instinct for well-placed ornament were often elaborately moulded, or chamfered and pierced with cusping or tracery; not many are left now, owing to their exposed position. Fig. 25 shows a fine example

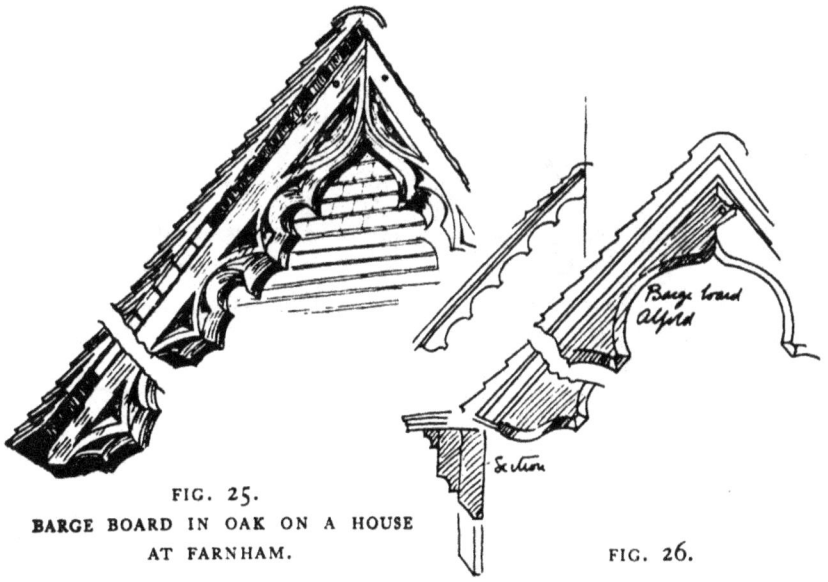

FIG. 25.
BARGE BOARD IN OAK ON A HOUSE AT FARNHAM.

FIG. 26.

on a house facing the church at Farnham, and Plate LXXV shows the original large board at the Post Office at Shamley Green. Fig. 26 is from Alfold; Plate XIX the detail view of the porch at Crossways Farm, Abinger, shows a moulded board, the moulding agreeably mitred and returned at the bottom.

The "healing," or roof covering itself, was originally of thatch of reed or straw, or of wooden shingles. I know of no roof of wood shingles in Surrey, though they still exist in other parts of the country. Thatch is fast disappearing in Surrey. During the fourteenth century thatch was frequently whitewashed as a precaution against fire.[1] The danger from fire, and the cost of up-keep, both play their part in eliminating thatch, but its disappearance is chiefly owing to machine reaping, which so bruises the straw that its life is only one-third of that reaped by hand; hand reaping is now almost a thing of the past, so that thatching is in danger of becoming a lost art. Roofs of Horsham stone slates are frequently found in Surrey;

FIG. 27.

the slates are laid in diminishing courses, the big ones at the eaves, and the smallest at the apex of the roof; the pitch of the roof is generally less steep on account of the weight of the material, and the consequent stress on the wooden pins holding the stone slate. These pins perish in time, and it is probable that all the examples of stone roofing shown in these illustrations have been relaid at one time or another. No doubt when these removals took place, the stone was often replaced with tiles, as at Summersbury Farmhouse (Plate xxx). The pitch of the roof was generally, though not always, greater than 45°, avoiding a right angle in the gable, which

[1] Parker's *History of Domestic Architecture*.

is not pleasant in this position. As an exception to this rule I note that Puttenden and Bonnet's Farm at Ockley (Plate LXI) appear to be roofed at an angle of 45°. The latter has a stone roof, but it illustrates my point in favour of an acute angle for a gable. The angle of the guest house at Lingfield, which is stone roofed, (Plate L) is about 47°, as also is that of the cottage at Frensham (Fig. 15).

The tiled roofs and walls now seen in so many houses are

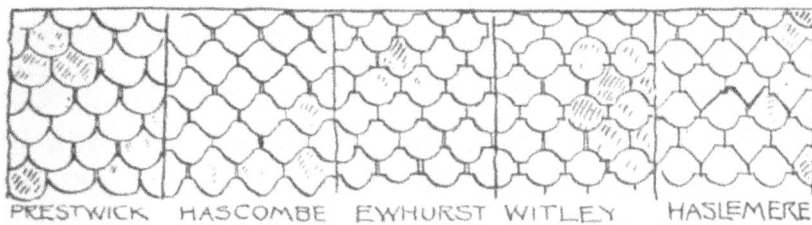

FIG. 28. EXAMPLES OF WEATHER TILING.

not, except in late examples, the original covering. In the fifteenth, sixteenth, and seventeenth centuries there was a great demand for tiles to replace roofs of wooden shingles or thatch, and it was only when the supply was more than sufficient for the demands of more important personages that the yeoman and the cottager could come by them.[1] The earliest tiles were probably rounded, like the scale of a fish, as illustrated in MS. of the period, and not straight. I know of only

[1] "The art of working clay, one of the earliest arts, never fell wholly into abeyance in any country in which it had been extensively practised. In England it survived the period of Roman dominion, during which it was extensively cultivated; in the Domesday Survey potters appear among other crafts incidentally enumerated."— Turner, p. xxvii.

Tiles and bricks and glass were imported from abroad in the thirteenth and fourteenth centuries, and foreign craftsmen were recruited abroad to forward the home industries.

one cottage roofed entirely with these rounded tiles, about two miles south of Redhill, and cannot say whether they are original or the freak of a later period. This pattern is seen in vertical tile hanging at Prestwick (Fig. 28) and elsewhere. Figure 28 shows other fancy shaped tiles used for vertical tile hanging in various combinations; neither on a roof nor on a wall, as weather tiling, do fancy shaped tiles, in my opinion, look so well as the straight. Fig. 29 shows a pattern on the old mill at Shalford. Perhaps the most satisfactory patterns are those produced by using straight-edged tiles of different colours in various forms of diaper. The tiles for this purpose were sometimes of the same make and colour when they left the potter's hands, the pattern developing only with age; one lot of the tiles forming the pattern had been dabbed with the bristles of a stiff brush before the tile was burnt, thus producing a rough surface which weathered more quickly than the ordinary hand-made tile. There are several reasons why an old tile roof looks better than a new, apart from the colour given to them by age and mossy growth. The tiles were thicker and more uneven in thickness and in size than are the tiles produced by modern machinery (though happily hand-made tiles are again easily procurable); the holing for the tile pins being done by hand was irregularly spaced; the laths were of rent oak and consequently very uneven; and the rafters were

FIG. 29.

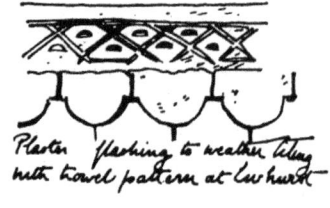

FIG. 30.

either pit sawn, or squared with the adze; the surface on which the tiles were laid was therefore an uneven one to start with, and time has warped and twisted them still further. I do not suggest that these attractive wavy lines should be reproduced in new work; to attempt it would be an unpardonable affectation, but the hand-made tile should be used, and the maker should not be asked to produce them too even in colour and thickness; the sand-faced hand-made tile will weather the delightful colour of the old roofs in due time. The old tiles were fastened with pins of hazel or willow, and sometimes of elder.[2] Weather tiles were hung on oak laths and were bedded

FIG. 31.

solid in lime and hair mortar. Fig. 30 shows the pattern worked in the plaster flashing with the bricklayer's trowel on a cottage at Ewhurst.

One of the features to be learned from old tiling is the saddle-back hip tiles at the salient junction of two planes of the roof. They form a rounder and more pleasing line at the hip than the right-angled tiles generally used to-day and they are to be had from most of the best tile makers. The gablet at the apex of hipped roofs is also an attractive feature of the old work; both gablet and hip tiles are shown on the frontispiece. The ridge tiles on the old roofs are

[1] Addy, p. 49.
[2] Nevill.

plain half-round tiles, which have not been improved upon since. I have seen and sketched ornamental ridge tiles in Suffolk, the individual work of one man, not a casting from a machine, but I know of none in Surrey. The practice of bedding roofing tiles in clean straw is still followed in some parts of Surrey, but in better-class work roofs are now always covered with boarding and felt before laying the tiles.

During the sixteenth century and the early part of the seven-

FIG. 32. NEWARK MILL, NEAR RIPLEY.

teenth, timber was the staple building material of the neighbourhood. Its use accounts in part for the disappearance of earlier work. A far larger number of the houses illustrated in this book are of timber framed construction than appears on the surface of the illustrations. From time to time repairs were undertaken, and defective walls were preserved by covering them with weather boarding [1] or

[1] The mill at Ripley (Fig. 32) is an instance on a large scale of a timber-framed building covered with weather boarding, probably at the time it was built.

IN SURREY

vertical tile hanging, or the whole front was plastered over and whitewashed. This was probably the case with the picturesque group of houses in the Farnham Road at Guildford (Fig. 31). The making of tiles was an industry which developed slowly, and there was a great demand for them for roofing, so that vertical tile hanging

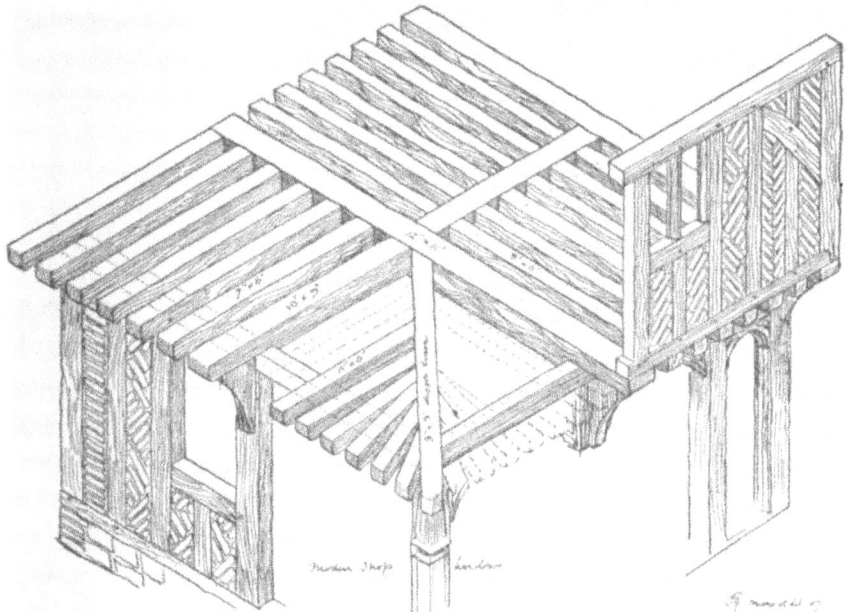

FIG. 33. OVERSAILING STORY OF SHOP IN LINGFIELD.

is generally of later date than most of the houses to which it has been applied. Stone was to be had, and a certain number of houses were built entirely of stone (Plate LXXXII and Fig. 8), but in general it was used in walls for foundations only, until brickfields were well established. Brick was first used almost entirely for chimneys; it was used then in conjunction with timber framing for filling in the panels (Fig. 33); later the ground floor was built of brick with timber framing above (Plates II and XLVII), and, as timber became scarcer, brick sup-

FIG. 34. DETAIL OF ANGLE POST, BREWER STREET FARM.

planted it for outer walls altogether (Plates xc and c). Later on I refer in more detail to brickwork.

The method of timber framing is extremely simple, and has been ably described in previous volumes of this series. The earliest type is that known as Post and Pan, the post being approximately the same size as the panel. Examples of this are shown on Plates xx, xxviii, and xli, illustrating a house at Ewhurst, Crowhurst, and Unstead. Sometimes the upright puncheons or quarters are ploughed and a board inserted between them as a panel, as in the rooms at Crowhurst Place. A section through them is shown in Fig. 41. The external wall is formed of a series of upright posts tenoned into a sill on or above the ground floor level and into a head at the ceiling level; the intervening spaces were filled with wattle and daub, a plaster of lime and loam mixed with chopped straw in it.[1] This adhered to the network of hazel bands

[1] A material not unlike Devonshire "cob," though I believe there is no lime in "cob."

previously fastened between the oak posts, which were grooved for this purpose. This wattle and daub basketwork must be a survival of primitive hut construction; it still stands in the

FIG. 35. DOORWAY AT BREWER STREET FARM.

gamekeeper's cottage at Frensham (Fig. 15) and in many other houses. Sometimes the filling was done with bricks laid in a herring-bone pattern, producing the beautiful effects illustrated in Plates LI and XXVIII at Lingfield and Ewhurst. The early

Post and Pan type is retained in superior work where the corbelling out of the upper story is adopted. I have made a rough diagram (Fig. 33) to illustrate these projecting stories, measured from the fine example at Lingfield. This was built about 1520

FIG. 36. BRAMLEY.

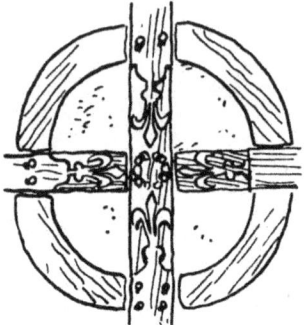

FIG. 37. DETAIL OF PANEL OF FIG. 44.

and would seem to have been a shop from the first; unfortunately it has been badly restored. Various reasons are given for thrust-

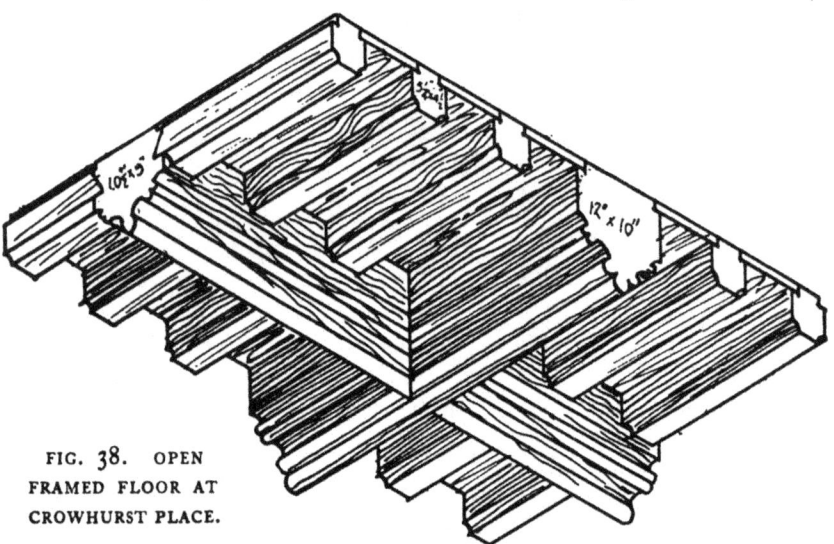

FIG. 38. OPEN FRAMED FLOOR AT CROWHURST PLACE.

IN SURREY

ing the upper story out over the lower, all of them more or less unlikely; it seems to me one of those developments which would arise on the spot while the work was in progress, justifiable alike on the score of sound construction, the economical use of material, and beauty of design. Take the instance of the farm at Brewer Street (Plate VIII). The dragon beam, corner post, struts and cantilever joist construction shown in more detail in Figs. 34 and 35, add greatly to

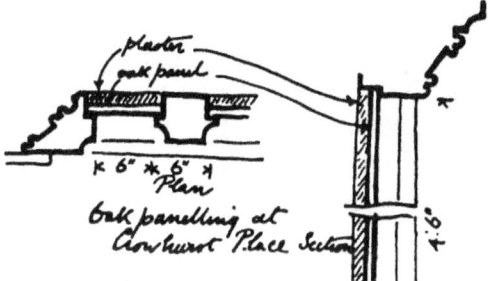

FIG. 41.

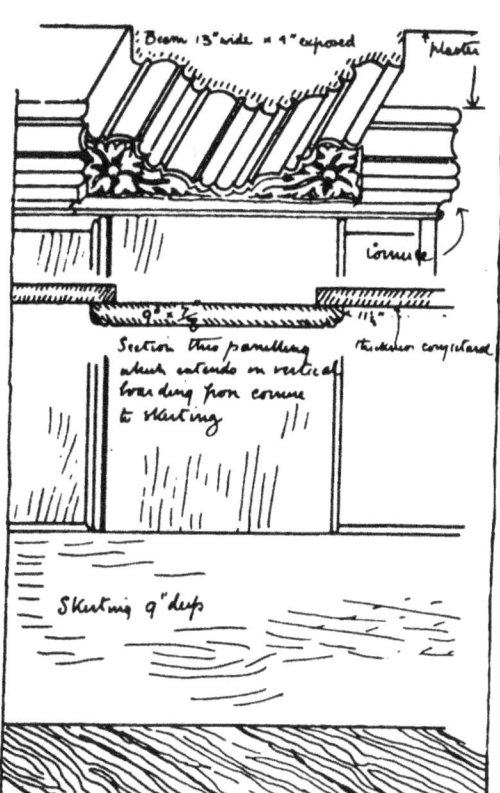

FIG. 39. BEAM AND PANELLING, REDE PLACE.

FIG. 40. HOUSE AT GODSTONE.

FIG. 42. THE "CROWN INN" AT CHIDDINGFOLD.

the stability of a form of construction none too weighty in itself; it allows of the use of short lengths of timber; it gives character to the design.

From the post and panel treatment, more complex systems were evolved, such as placing the timbers further apart, putting braces or struts to stiffen the frame, and forming small rectangular panels by the addition of transomes which were filled with ornamental struts.

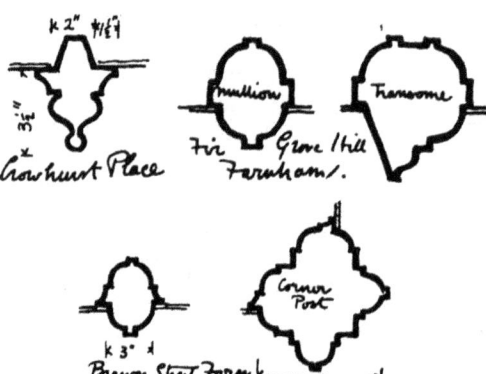

FIG. 43. TYPICAL WOODEN MOULDINGS.

The house at Shamley Green (Plates LXXIV–V) is a good example of the large panel treatment with curved braces. The most

FIG. 44. DETAIL OF WINDOW, GREAT TANGLEY.

elaborate is that at Great Tangley (Plates LXXXV–VI), the panels being treated with curved braces in the form of simple tracery (Fig. 44); Fig. 37 shows the carving on the puncheons and transomes; a simple treatment of the same forms is seen at Bramley. This treatment is carried to great lengths in other counties, but I think the more sober forms are preferable in every way. The oak in these half-timber houses has usually weathered a most delightful silver-grey colour; the blackened timbers have been treated artificially and are hard and unpleasant in comparison with the natural colour.

Many of the framed floors in buildings of timber construction are beautiful pieces of work; the mouldings of the joists and beams at Crowhurst, shown in the accompanying cut (Fig. 38) are extraordinarily refined. The less ornate mouldings are frequently quite as attractive, such as those at Rede Place (Fig. 39) and at Godstone (Fig. 40). These both rest on corbels simply carved, giving interest where it is wanted without any display of effort. The solid panelled walls at Crowhurst (Fig. 41) and Rede Place (Fig. 39) are also interesting, the panelling forming the wall being itself sufficiently strong to bear its share of the weight of the floor over.

FIG. 45.
MOULDINGS AND BRACKET OF WINDOW AT FARNHAM.

This is perhaps the place to speak of doors and windows and other joinery found in timber-built houses. Both doors and windows are openings left between the puncheons and transomes of the timber construction. Where these openings were moulded they were worked by hand on the solid posts of the house. During the fourteenth and fifteenth centuries windows were usually fitted with wooden shutters, the opening being guarded by square bars of oak or iron let into head and sill. Remains of these openings are to be seen at Lingfield and elsewhere. Glazed windows of the thirteenth and fourteenth centuries were rare and costly; a nobleman travelling from one of his houses to another would unhang his glazed casements and take them with him, together with his tapestry for shutting out draughts, his beds and other furniture. The *Crown Inn* at Chiddingfold (Fig. 42) shows the primitive window opening in the quarters of the timber construction; a slight rebate is cut for the iron casement and the fixed glazing; the

IN SURREY

FIG. 46. BAY WINDOW, HIGH STREET, GUILDFORD.

casements are hung on hooks driven into the posts. The charm of old joinery, apart from its fresh and direct design, lies in the hand-worked mouldings with which it is enriched. Nearly all the early window frames which remain are moulded — moulded out of English oak by hand labour. Fig. 43 gives sections of some of the mouldings used. The example from the Farnham window is the most common; that from Crowhurst Place is the only one of its kind I have seen; those of the windows at Great Tangley and Brewer Street are typical of the best sixteenth century work. A view of the Great Tangley window is given in Fig. 44, from a photograph taken by Mr. Davie.

Not many instances of transomed windows occur in these plates; they are found in work of a larger character than is here generally dealt with. In smaller work the lowness of the rooms prohibit the

FIG. 47.
BAY WINDOW, HIGH STREET, GUILDFORD.

higher form of window. Many of the old windows have been pulled out for larger lights of inferior work and design. Here and there the little old window frames are left in and built up, and larger ones added alongside. This applies very generally to bedrooms, once lit in an inadequate way, low down near the floor; the majority of dormer windows are additions to remedy this defect. West End Farm-house, near Chiddingfold (Plate XII), shows the long stretch of glazing so characteristic of Tudor work. A modified instance of this at Great Tangley is shown on Plate LXXXVI. Summersbury Farmhouse (Fig. 16) shows the horizontal treatment of glazing between the puncheons supporting the building.

FIG. 48.
BAY WINDOW, GUILDFORD.

Plate xxxv includes a view of a window in a gable of a house on Fir Grove Hill, Farnham, an early and favourite form of cottage window, of which few are now left. Fig. 45 shows the mouldings and simple carving on the bracket, sill and head of this window.

Bay windows are not a characteristic feature of early work. Those shown in Figs.

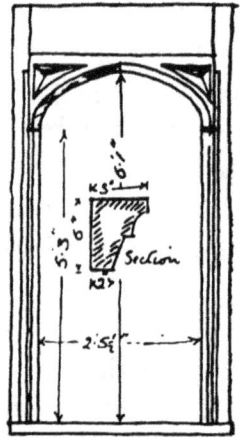

FIG. 49.
AT BREWER STREET.

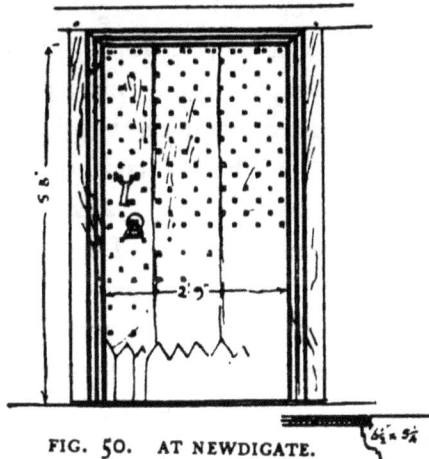

FIG. 50. AT NEWDIGATE.

46, 47, 48, date probably from the seventeenth and eighteenth centuries. They are without the grace and strength of earlier joinery, but they are pleasing features in the Guildford High Street, with the exception perhaps of Castle Street, Farnham (Plate XXXIV), the most picturesque street in Surrey. These illustrate the flat section of frame and mullion of later work, which is perhaps the most suitable section at the present time.

Fig. 49 shows a door opening at Brewer Street Farm-house—a common type in the sixteenth century—this is an inner frame with no sign of a door; probably a tapestry or leather hanging was used. Doors are exposed perhaps to more wear and tear than any other part of the house, and it is not surprising that the number of original doors, or "claddings," as they were called, should be few and far between. The original frames are of substantial timbers, usually about 6 inches

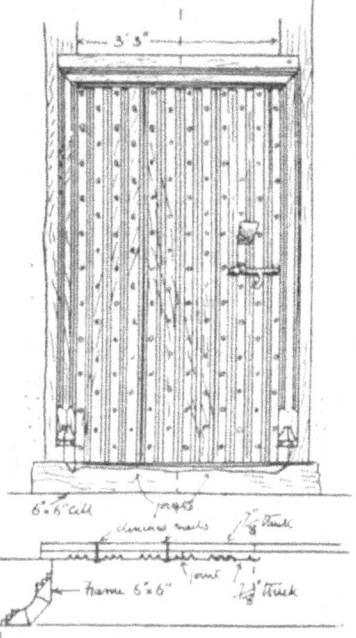

FIG. 51. HALF PLAN AND SECTION THROUGH FRAME DOOR AND FRAME, PUTTENDEN.

40 OLD COTTAGES AND FARM-HOUSES

FIG. 52.
DOOR AT ABBOT'S HOSPITAL, GUILDFORD.

square, with a large plain or moulded chamfer, with a simple but effectively designed stop on the inner arris on the outerside of the door; Figs. 51, 52 are instances of this. The doorpost at the Brewer Street Farm-house measures 16¼ inches × 13 inches, which, as far as I know, is only surpassed in bulk by story posts. That supporting the dragon beam at the same farm is out of timber about 36 inches × 16 inches, set root uppermost.

The doors at Newdigate and Puttenden are made of two thicknesses of oak, the outer one vertical, the inner one horizontal, secured together by rough wrought-

FIG. 53.
BACK ENTRANCE, WOLVENS FARM.

IN SURREY

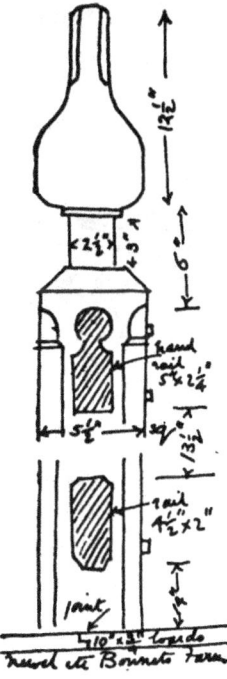

FIG. 54.

iron nails long enough to be driven through both thicknesses of board and clenched on the inner side. The outer side is often of moulded boarding, as in Figs. 51, 52; the inner is usually quite plain, the clenched nail points are exposed to view, the hinges, latch, and bolts, where they are original, make the inner face pleasing to the eye. The joints in the internal boarding in some cases were covered with plain moulded strips some 2½ inches wide and ¾ inch thick.

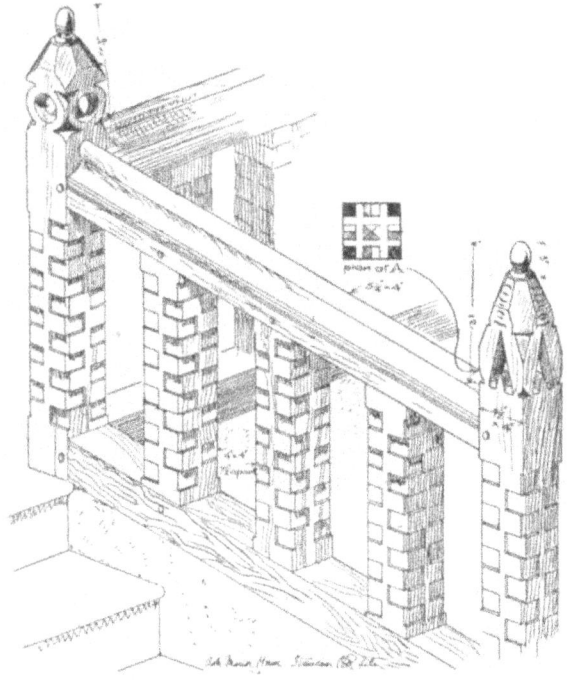

FIG. 55. ASH MANOR FARM STAIRCASE.

No less vigorous are other details of joinery. The newel post and handrail to the stair at Bonnet's Farm (Fig. 54), and the admirable newels, handrails and balusters at Ash Manor Farm (Fig. 55), are typical examples of this class of work. In

42   OLD COTTAGES AND FARM-HOUSES

neither do the original treads and risers remain. The extremely slow rise of the balustrade at Ash Manor Farm, having no con-

FIG. 56.   OAK TRESTLE TABLE AND BENCHES AT BONNET'S FARM, OCKLEY.

nection with the rise of the existing stair, suggests that there may once have been an inclined slope, such as are found in houses on the Continent, or a very shallow stair cut from the solid log. These are both instances from yeomen's houses of the best class (*see* Plates IV and LXI). The early cottages either had no stair,

FIG. 57.   TABLE AND BENCH AT ABBOT'S HOSPITAL, GUILDFORD.

the upper rooms being reached by a ladder, or the stair was cut out of a solid plank, or it was formed of winders around a

IN SURREY

FIG. 58. FIRESIDE SETTLE AT ABBOT'S HOSPITAL, GUILDFORD.

central massive newel post.

Fig. 56 shows the seating arrangements at Bonnet's Farm. Chairs would be almost unknown in these houses at the time they were built. Fig. 57 shows a more ornate table and stool from Abbot's Hospital at Guildford; from which place I drew the fireside settle (Fig. 58). The chest (Fig. 59) is a good instance of the simple ornament of the joiner's trade; the joiner was also responsible for the early dinner service shown in Fig. 60, though tradition says that a large piece of bread was more generally used than a wooden plate.

These timber-built houses are, I am afraid, an art of the past. When they were built, they were the natural product of the country side. Now the oak forests are gone, and no fresh trees are

FIG. 59. CHEST, STOKE D'ABERNON CHURCH.

planted; instead of timber being the material common to all, it is only the wealthiest who can afford to use it with that careless generosity of bulk which characterizes the old work, and makes it so agreeable and satisfying to the eye. Moreover, we have building bye-laws in many country places suitable only for crowded towns, which necessitate a brick backing to the timber construction, of a thickness rendering the timber unnecessary for constructional purposes. These building bye-laws are much in need of reform in country places, in so far as they lay down the law on matters purely architectural. Those that relate to the height of rooms often impose height greater than that which is desirable for health in cottages, and which is destructive of all proportion in small rooms, and needlessly extravagant of material.

FIG. 60. OLD WOODEN PLATTERS.

Enlightened model bye-laws are nowadays a necessity, and, like the system of building by contract, are a far older institution than many people imagine. Instances of both, dating from the thirteenth century, are given in Turner's *Domestic Architecture of the Middle Ages*.

The brick-built houses in this book are generally of later date than those of timber, and as brick, where it is easily obtainable, as it is in Surrey, is the cheapest building material, these brick-built cottages have a special interest for us to-day.

The earliest use of brick in this country since the Roman occupation is a matter of controversy at the present time; it has hitherto been generally supposed that bricks were re-introduced into England by the Flemish weavers who settled here in the fifteenth century; they are supposed to have imported bricks direct from Holland. Mr. John Bilson, writing in the *R.I.B.A. Journal* of January 11, 1908, takes the view that bricks were being made in England, and had been made for a long time before this date. Mr. Bilson points out that they were known as tiles in this country until the fifteenth century; either as "wall-tiles," which came to be called bricks, or "thack-tiles" (roofing tiles).

FIG. 61.

The Flemish immigrants may well have been acquainted with the beautiful brickwork of the Netherlands, and they may have imported skilled brickmakers from that country to encourage the manufacture of bricks, and the art of building in them.

In Surrey, brickwork was at first confined to chimneys; it was then used in place of plaster and wattle for filling in the space between the timbers of framed houses; and by the time of Charles I. it had become the staple building material.

The old bricks are a better shape than the standard size now made. They are longer in proportion to their thickness; those in the gamekeeper's cottage at Frensham are a very average size; they vary, but are about 10 inches × 5 inches × 2⅛ inches. 2 inches to 2¼ inches is the usual thickness. They are very hard and rough, and uneven in shape and size. The mortar joint is wide, and greatly adds to the good appearance of the wall. The local bricks of Surrey are, as a rule, excessively porous when first made, but the surface becomes harder with time. It is only partly true that the colour of a brick depends upon the clay of which it is made; it is more a matter of the amount of heat it undergoes in the process of burning.

The modern practice of importing machine-made bricks for external facings destroys all interest in the surface of the wall; they set up a false standard for the bricklayer, and it is, besides, well known that for weathering purposes a local material will often stand better than that imported from a distance.

There is, as far as I know, nothing to be said in favour of using bricks of machine-like evenness of shape and colour. Such bricks, too thick in proportion to their length, laid with a thin starved-looking joint, make an ugly and lifeless wall, a thing unsightly to look at and difficult to cover. The important thing is that the bricks should be hard and well burnt, the rougher they are the better will the mortar adhere; the joints in the brickwork are a pleasing relief to the wall surface, provided they are of lime mortar and not of Portland cement; if good lime and sharp gritty sand of uneven grains be used for the mortar, its life will be as good, and it will become as hard, as the brick itself. In domestic work, Portland cement in place of lime is both extravagant and undesirable, unless for exceptional positions, and even then, is it not permissible to point the joints on good lime mortar.

Chimneys were one of the first parts of a house to be built in brick. Parker gives an extract from the household book of a Sir John Howard in the fifteenth century, showing the cost of adding a chimney to be twenty-six shillings. The fire originally burnt in a metal brazier standing in the centre of the room, the smoke escaping from an outlet in the apex of the roof. This was often the case down to the middle of the sixteenth century. The flues formed in the thickness of the wall of Bolton Castle were noticed by Leland in 1538 as something curious and remarkable, and no doubt they existed in the castle long before they did in the yeoman's house or the cottage. Such a primitive arrangement could only have been possible with wood fires, and must have been very uncomfortable for the occupants.[1] When the open roofed central hall or common room was converted into rooms one over the other, as was the case at Great Tangley and

FIG. 62.   NEAR HASLEMERE.

---

[1] Coal was introduced into London in the fourteenth century; the citizens objected strongly to its use as it blackened the external walls of their whitewashed houses.

the guest house at Lingfield, flues to carry the smoke became not a luxury but a necessity. This multiplication of chimneys in the better class houses dates from the fifteenth century.[1]

The chimneys built outside the houses of early date have all the appearance of additions, particularly in houses of timber construction. In the smaller examples, the stacks usually occur at the end of the house, sometimes, as at Milford (Plate LIII), there is one at either end, and very charming is the effect so obtained; nevertheless it is a position to be adopted in modern work with circumspection, requiring, as it does, considerable skill and

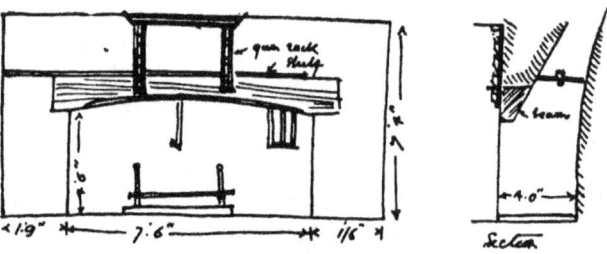

FIG. 63. FIREPLACE AT GODSTONE.

judgment where the size of the stack may have to be relatively small. In other instances, again, the stack is built up inside the existing building, as at the guest house at Lingfield, emerging sometimes astride the ridge and sometimes to one side of it, as at Eashing (Plate XXII). The treatment of the roof in this example so as to avoid a gutter is very characteristic; so far as I know it has died out in this country, but it is still practised in France.

The internal chimney stack gives greater warmth to the house than the fireplace built in an outer wall.

The chimney corner within (Fig. 65) and the stack without

[1] Turner, *Domestic Architecture of the Middle Ages.*

IN SURREY

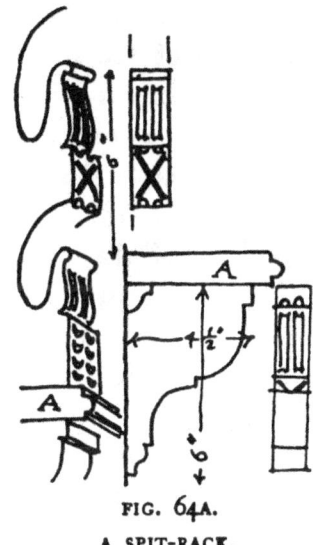

FIG. 64A.
A SPIT-RACK.

(Fig. 62) are among the most delightful features of the Surrey cottage. The chimney corner was a natural development of the requirements of the time. Wood was the only fuel, and it was to be had for the gathering, in great abundance. Parker says it was thrown on the fire in alternate layers of dry and green faggots. The hearth therefore was large and the canopy overspreading and capacious, to collect and carry the smoke. The recess was the most convenient form, the opening as low as possible to prevent the smoke eddying out into the room; that at Godstone (Fig. 63) shows the simplest form of open fire. The lintel was usually a chamfered oak beam roughly squared with the adze, though occasionally a four-centred or semi-elliptical brick arch was turned over the opening, as at Holdfast Farm, near Haslemere. The sizes of the recess vary in the smaller examples, generally not less than 3 feet 6 inches deep, and some-

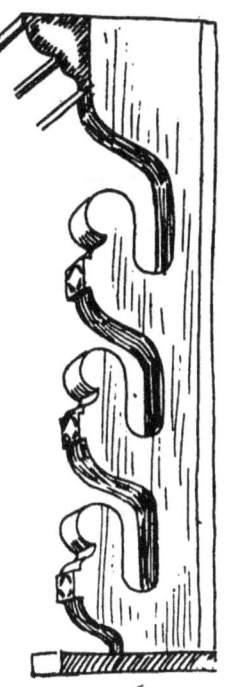

FIG. 64B.
A SPIT-RACK.

times as much as 10 feet 6 inches wide; the gathering in of the canopy to the flue externally forms a series of tile roofed offsets which give grace and beauty to the base of the stack. Occasionally the tiled roofs over these offsets are stopped by parapet walls in the form of brick corbie steps, so common in the gables of brick-built houses in the eastern counties; instances of this occur at Unstead, and are shown on Plate XLII.

FIG. 65. STAIRS FROM THE UPPER STORY, CROWHURST PLACE.

The windows sometimes found in these recesses are of later date and are not generally satisfactory additions. The cooking was done at the open fire, and the master of the house could, at the end of the day, betake himself to the seat within the fireplace, and there enjoy his pipe. When the recess continues through the upper floor the bacon was hung and smoked in the great open chimney. Now, alas, the open fire is old-fashioned, and few remain in their original state.

The hearth itself was of brick, raised its own thickness above the floor level; the fine cast-iron firebacks of the Weald protected

FIG. 66. CROWHURST PLACE: INTERIOR OF ROOM OVER PARLOUR.

the bricks where the fire was hottest; on the hearth stood fire dogs for supporting the heavier logs, an iron bracket built into the wall to support the kettle or pot, and oak seats on either side of the fire, supported on brickwork completed the inner side of the recess; over the lintel would be a rack (Fig 64) from which was suspended the spit for roasting, and then a shelf, possibly furnished with polished brass and pewter and earthenware; beneath the lintel a narrow printed

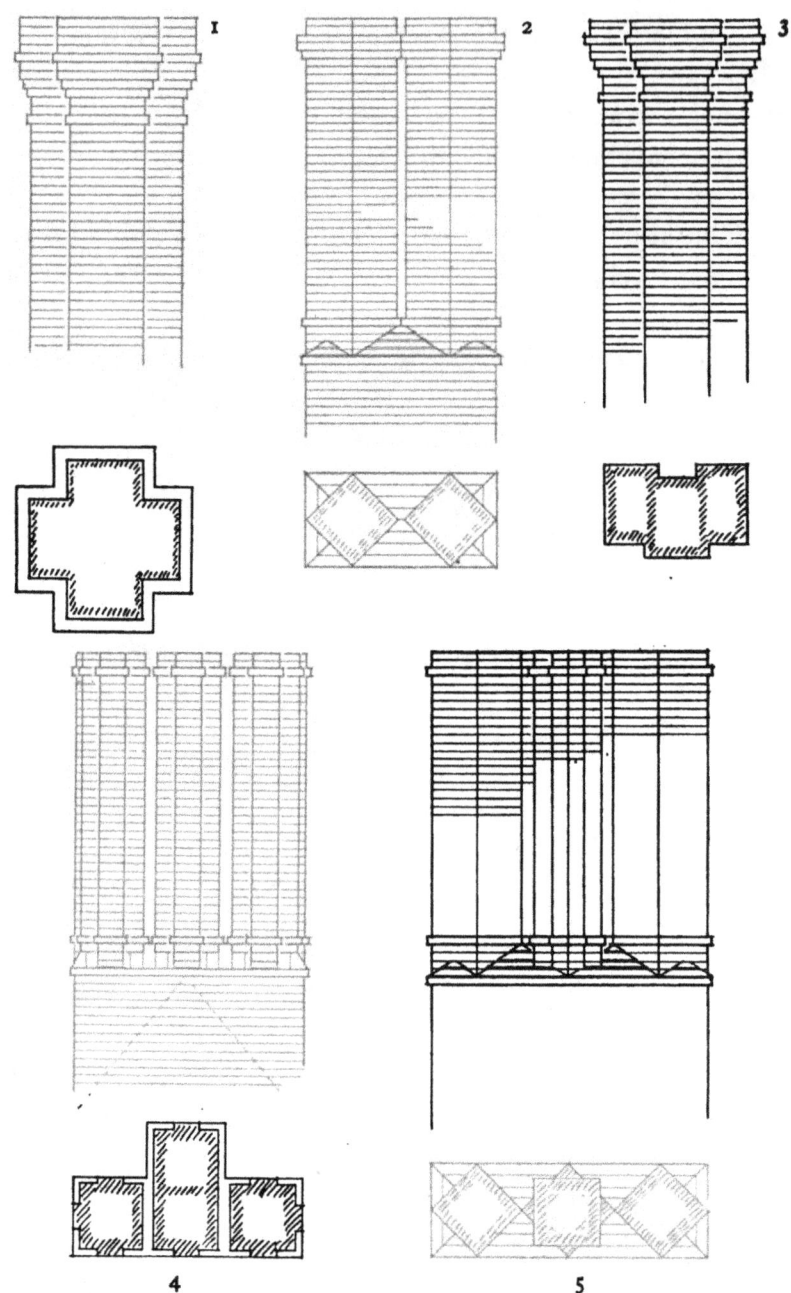

FIG. 67. NOS. 1–5. TYPICAL FORMS OF CHIMNEYS: 1, FROM HASLEMERE; 2, FROM FARNCOMBE; 4 AND 5, FROM GOMSHALL.

IN SURREY

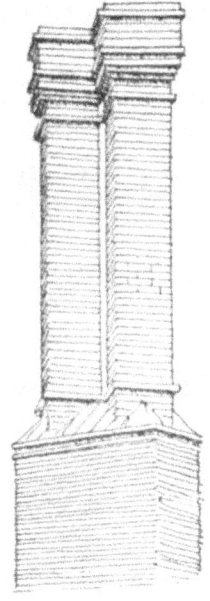

FIG. 68. AT BONNET'S FARM, OCKLEY.

cotton curtain was hung, to assist in keeping back the smoke. Each accessory was pleasing in itself, and the decoration of the room was entirely dependent upon that which was necessary and useful.

Figs. 65 and 66 illustrate interiors at Crowhurst Place, both good examples of a fifteenth-century interior entirely of timber, with the exception of the fireplace, and containing many wrought beams.

The variety of treatment of the chimney stacks themselves is almost endless, and it is not easy to find two exactly alike, except in the same village. The chimney on the external wall has generally two flues only, that of the kitchen and that of the room over;

FIG. 69. AT SHOTTERMILL.

often there is only the one. In late work many more fireplaces were required, and the stacks, whether on external walls, or emerging through the roof, rise in a great mass of masonry high above the level of the roof. Occasionally the flues are contained in separate shafts rising from the same base, which give

FIG. 70. ASH MANOR FARM.

FIG. 71. RAKE HOUSE.

lightness and beauty to the whole. More frequently many flues are built in one stack, sometimes regular (Fig. 71) and sometimes irregular in plan (Figs. 69, 70). The plainest of these give a certain distinction to the building from the large and generous part they play in the general design. Those at Bonnet's Farm and Rake

House (Figs. 68 and 71) are things of beauty, and a joy for ever. If we cannot achieve the more ornate we can at least see that our houses have the distinction of the simpler treatment; gathering as many flues as possible into one stack rather than multiplying the number of stacks makes for economy in building, and efficiency in carrying the smoke and keeping the house warm. The examples I have drawn are given without a scale. The position renders it out of the question to measure them with a foot rule, and though the bricks and the jointing have been carefully counted, the size of the bricks varies too much for it to be safe to add a scale of feet and inches. The flues seem to vary in size, though they appear to be never less than 9 inches × 14 inches, sometimes a great deal more. From the jointing of the brickwork the outer skin appears seldom to be more than half a brick thick above the base of the shaft, after it emerges through the roof. In good work of the present day, the outer wall of a stack is generally one brick thick, with the consequence that our flues draw better than our ancestors' did, though this is not the only reason. An attractive addition to the old stack is sometimes found in the large bake ovens built on at its base, covered with a lean-to roof, such as those shown on Plates XXIII and LXXX. I do not know the date of the first chimney pot; many old chimneys have rudely constructed pots, conical in shape, of brick plastered over; and some have roofs of brick and tile, locally called a "bonnet." The

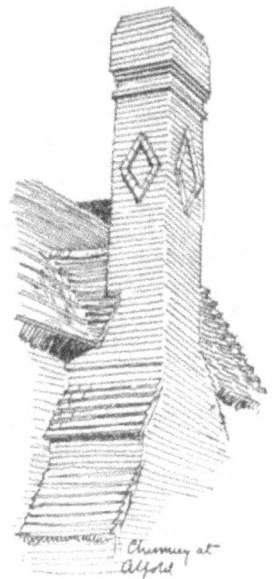

FIG. 72.

details of the chimney stacks are of the simplest character; even in the richest examples the designs are not laboured, but the expression of material rightly used.

Indeed, Surrey is happy in the purity of style both of brickwork and of half-timber construction: neither makes any extravagant display of ornamental detail such as characterizes some of the brick building of the eastern counties, and the half-timber work of the Midlands. Wherever detail does not assist the main object of the building it is excluded, and where it is called for it is appropriate to the material and of good workmanship.

FIG. 73. GODALMING.

The exception to this general statement is to be found in instances of ornamental brickwork of the middle of the seventeenth century. The examples occur only, to my knowledge, in or near the important market towns of Farnham, Guildford, and Godalming, places where the fashion of foreign ways would first take hold in the country. The most successful of these is that of the old town hall in Farnham, of which the merest fragment remains. The lower wall surface was divided into bays by a rude representation of the Ionic order, supporting a cornice all of brick; a deep frieze over this to the eaves is panelled in alternate squares and circles. The examples at Godalming (Figs. 73, 74) are not of such happy

FIG. 74. GODALMING.

design, but show a lively fancy and enjoyment of the possibilities of the material; the panel in Fig. 74 is dated 1663. The iron window frames look of later date, and detract from the design by the pattern of the iron glazing bars, itself unobjectionable, but introducing in this instance a fresh element in an already restless piece of design. Happiest of all are the quiet brick mouldings and cornices found on the front of the Crossways Farm near Abinger (Plate XIX), and in some small houses in Guildford. I think

FIG. 75.
COTTAGE IN FARNHAM.

the charm of the delightful cottage at Milford, shown on Plate LIII, is due to the general design rather than to the treatment of brick panelling on the front. In the seventeenth and eighteenth centuries, rubbed bricks for mouldings were used in chimneys, bases and heads and string courses (Figs. 61 and 75). Bricks were used for the window frames and mullions in place of wood, in imitation of the traditional stone treatment. The effect is not unpleasing, though the straight heads of the windows, strong as these are in practice in well executed work, is aesthetically unpardonable. In the almshouses at Farncombe (Plate XXXI and Fig. 78) this brickwork has unfortunately been painted white in imitation of stone, a deplorable piece of vandalism. A simple expedient for giving interest to a plain brick wall is that of using bricks of different colours forming a pattern in the wall. Plate V at Tongham, and Plate I at Alfold are examples of this. The bonding of the brickwork shows alternate "headers" (ends) and "stretchers" (sides) of the brick. The headers in these cottages are of a darker colour than the stretchers; very likely the bricks were from the same kiln, the headers more burnt than the stretchers.

FIG. 76.

IN SURREY

It will be noticed in the Godalming front that the plain surface, between the brick framing are filled with stone walling.

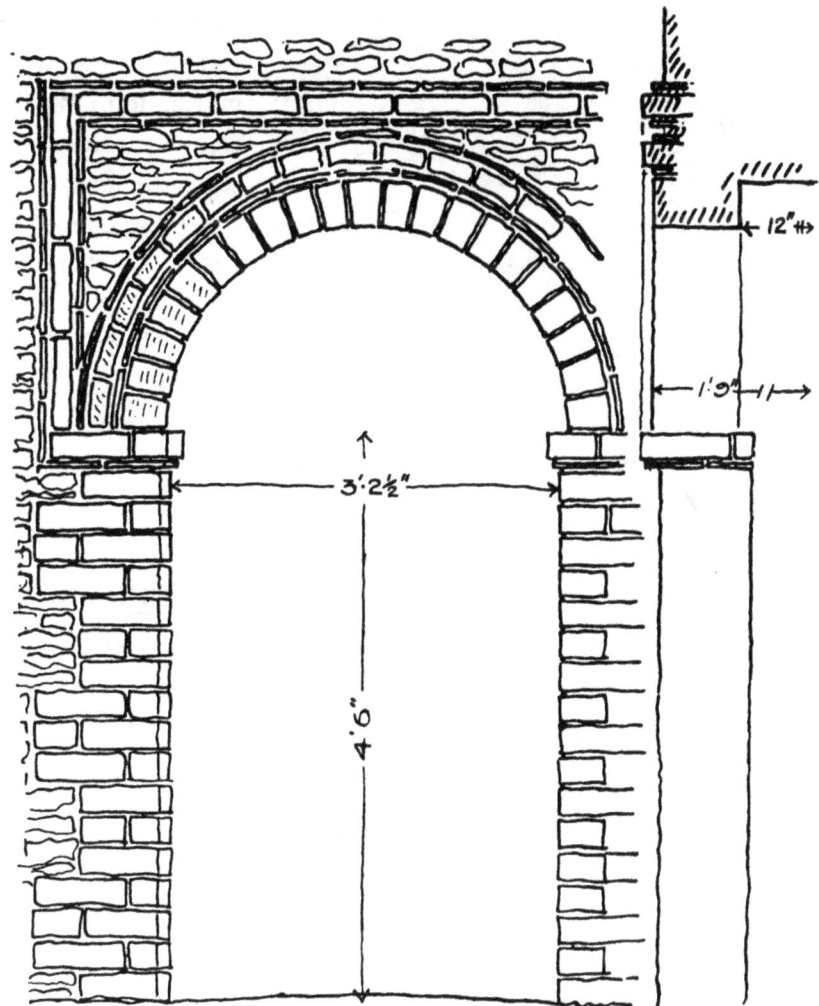

FIG. 77. GARDEN WALL DOORWAY, GREAT TANGLEY MANOR.

Bargate stone is used a great deal in the neighbourhood of Godalming. There are also stone cottages of the Tudor period in Hasle-

FIG. 78. ALMSHOUSES AT FARNCOMBE.

mere, and another example is shown on Plate LXXXII. A feature of the wide mortar joints in the masonry is the pressing in of small iron stones like nailheads, known as "galleting" or "garnetting (Fig 76).

The house at Ockley, otherwise brick built, has stone quoins to the chimney stacks; the lower part of the farm at Seale is of stone with brick dressings to the window openings (Fig. 76). Local rag stone was also largely used for foundations, though unfortunately these were often very inadequate. The wall enclosing the garden at Great Tangley Manor is a delightful combination of Bargate stone and brick and tile. Fig. 77 shows one of the little doorways in the wall; I do not know the date of this.

Plates XXXVI, LVIII, and others show groups

FIG. 79.

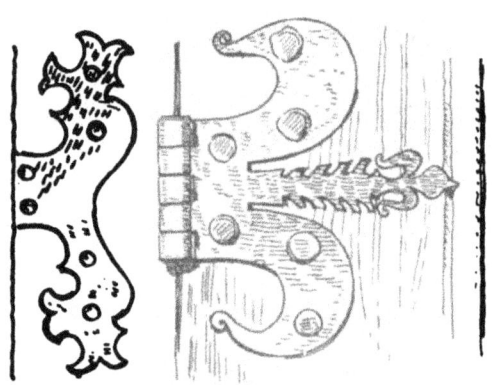

FIG. 80.

IN SURREY

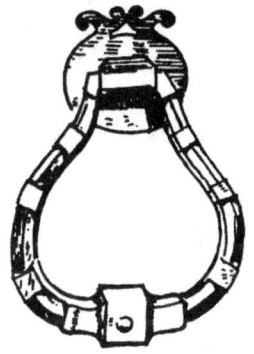

FIG. 81.
KNOCKER AT PUTTENDEN.

FIG. 82.

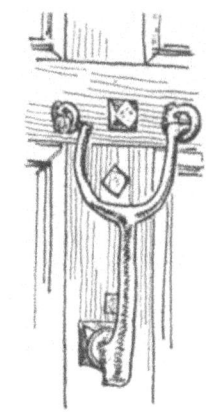

FIG. 83.
KNOCKER AT TANGLEY.

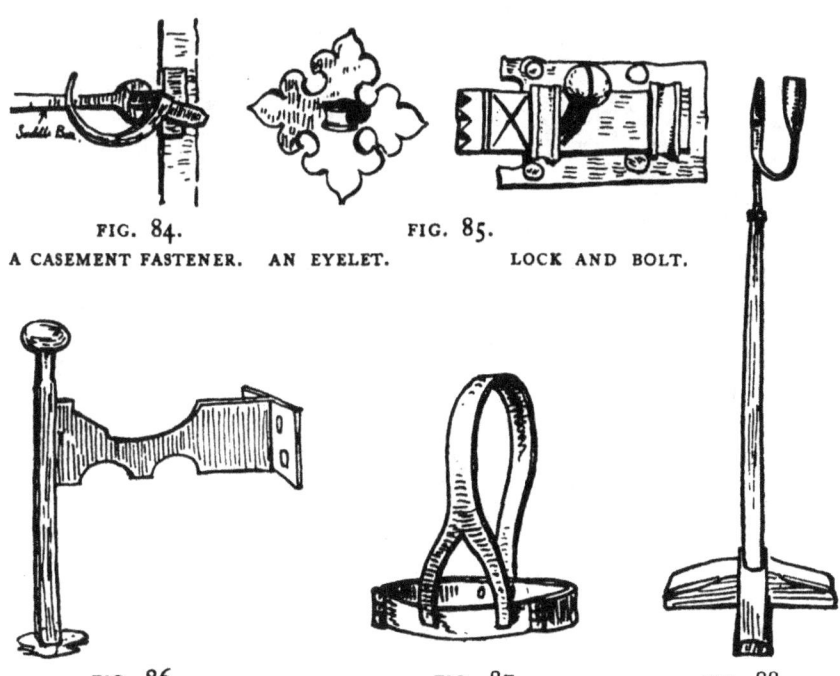

FIG. 84. A CASEMENT FASTENER. AN EYELET. FIG. 85. LOCK AND BOLT.

FIG. 86. FOOT SCRAPER. FIG. 87. SCOLD'S BRIDLE. FIG. 88. RUSHLIGHT HOLDER.

OLD METAL-WORK.

FIG. 89.
THE SIGN OF THE "WHITE HART," BLETCHINGLY.

of brick houses of quiet and unobtrusive design greatly preferable to the majority of modern houses of the same class.

This is not the place to consider the household gear and furniture of the old cottages; that has recently been done by an authority upon the subject. It is, however, within the architect's province to refer to the iron and lead work forming part of the house itself. It has been left to modern factories and modern civilization to produce, and condone, work in metal without either grace of workmanship or beauty of design. Within recent years enlightened craftsmen have set themselves to carry on the tradition of the smith; a few with such success as to reassure the most desponding lover of these crafts.

FIG. 90.
AN ENTRANCE GATEWAY IN FARNHAM.

Manuscripts from the tenth century onwards record ironwork, always of an ornamental character. Our museums house "little miracles of art" in metal. The name of *smith* was once honoured amongst the arts, when, as in the words of Keats—

To be first in beauty was to be first in might.

The common fittings about these old houses served—and where they remain still serve—to gratify the eye as well as honour the maker and his trade. Of household effects the most ingenious and most ornate were the chimney cranes, roasting spits and fire-dogs of the kitchen fire; these are now only to be found in museums. Besides compiling the valuable records in her book upon *Old West Surrey*, Miss Jekyll has formed a museum at Guildford, where the choicest examples of household effects may be seen.

FIG. 91. IRONWORK OF GATE SHOWN IN FIG. 90.

Hinges, richly foliated in the churches, plain, but with chequered tooled patterns in the houses, stretch their arms across the old doors; they served the double purpose of securing our ancestors against the outer world, and the doors themselves against the ravages of time (Figs. 79 and 80). The door handles and knockers (Figs. 81, 82, 83) were no doubt made in the village, and in work of any importance a temporary

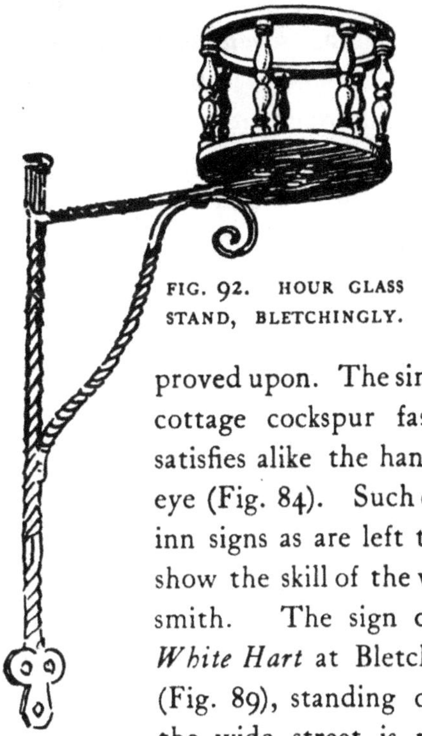

IN SURREY

forge would be set up on the spot, as in the thirteenth century.[1] Locks and bolts were legitimate opportunities for the craftsman's genius (Fig. 85). The casement fasteners of the sixteenth and seventeenth centuries at Guildford and elsewhere have still to be improved upon. The simplest cottage cockspur fastener satisfies alike the hand and eye (Fig. 84). Such of the inn signs as are left to-day show the skill of the village smith. The sign of the *White Hart* at Bletchingly (Fig. 89), standing out in the wide street, is not to be lightly passed. The figure of a heart is worked with taste into the design, framing the carved and painted bunch of grapes in its centre. Colouring and gilding was much used on iron, lead, and wood, and traces of it are still to be found in the more protected parts of the work.

FIG. 92. HOUR GLASS STAND, BLETCHINGLY.

FIG. 93. FARNHAM.

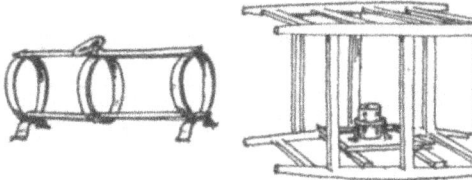

FIG. 94. PIPE RACK.   FIG. 95. BED WAGON.

[1] Turner.

66 OLD COTTAGES AND FARM-HOUSES

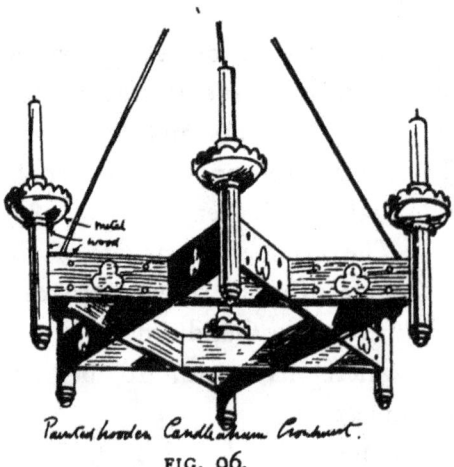

FIG. 96.

Better class houses of the seventeenth and eighteenth centuries were richly ornamented with the smith's art in gates and fences, grilles and fanlights; Figs. 90 and 91 are from a house in Castle Street, Farnham.

Casement frames have been bettered in recent years for weatherproof qualities; so too has the lead caning securing the small panes of glass. The flat wide section of the caning is still the best, but in good work it is made a little wider —not less than ½ inch—and the jointing is done with a weatherproof mastic. The early windows generally show the diamond-shaped quarries, and the later ones those of rectangular shape. The rectangular lines are the most restful from inside the room, and are to be preferred in new work; in neither do I know of cases of narrow borders such as are sometimes used nowadays, and I do not think their introduction is any improvement upon the old

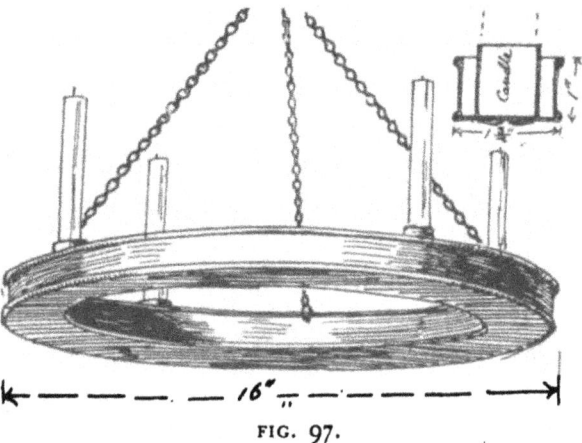

FIG. 97.
CANDELABRUM AT ABBOT'S HOSPITAL, GUILDFORD.

IN SURREY

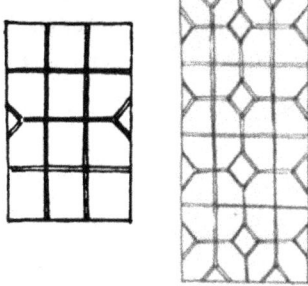

FIG. 98.
GLAZING AT
OXTED.

FIG. 99.
GLAZING AT
ALFOLD.

way. Although, as Mr. Nevill points out, the charming quality of the old glass is due to decay, it is possible to use discrimination in the choice of modern glass, the best "trade" qualities are by no means necessarily the most desirable. The practice of inserting large plate-glass windows is perhaps one of the most objectionable ever introduced into domestic architecture. The window opening unrelieved by the tracery of leaded lines, or even by the harder lines of wooden glazing bars, is a chilling blank; much as the human eye is when suffering from cataract; in-

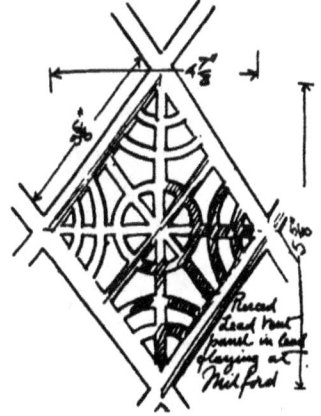

FIG. 100.

FIG. 101. LEAD RAINWATER
HEADS, GUILDFORD.

ternally the plate glass gives no sense of comfort or of being under the shelter of a roof. There were occasional excursions from the diamond or simple rectangular patterns; that shown on Fig. 98 from Oxted has the excuse of the saddlebar and fastener where the pattern is varied; Fig. 99 is from a cottage at Alfold. A quaint and delightful feature of these cottages is the ventilating lights with pierced patterns cast in lead, many of delicate lattice type. Examples are shown

FIG. 102. A WELL AT EASHING.

from Milford (Fig. 100), and an elaborate one from the dairy window of Summersbury Farm-house (Fig. 16).

Lead was a material cast and cut into endless beautiful forms. The three lead rainwater heads (Figs. 101 and 103) are all from Guildford; that from Abbot's Hospital is dated 1627; the others are probably later. I know of no instance of its use in cottages unless it be for pumps. Most of the cottages have their own wells, raising the water either with dippers or with a winch and bucket. Fig. 102 shows one of these well heads with a rough roof over it; the wooden buckets are now practically a thing of the past.

FIG. 103. RAINWATER HEAD AT ABBOT'S HOSPITAL, GUILDFORD.

Butler & Tanner, The Selwood Printing Works, Frome, and London.

Plate I.

AT ALFOLD.

Plate II.

BY THE CHURCH, ALFOLD.

IN ASH VILLAGE.

COTTAGES BY THE CHURCH, ALFOLD.

Plate IV.

ASH MANOR FARM.

THE VILLAGE STREET, ASH.

BETWEEN TONGHAM AND FARNHAM.

Plate VI.

COTTAGES, CHURCH GREEN, BEDDINGTON.

Plate VII.

COTTAGES, CHURCH GREEN, BEDDINGTON.

Plate VIII.

FARMHOUSE, BREWER STREET, BLETCHINGLY.

Plate IX.

COTTAGES, IN VILLAGE NEAR CHURCH.

Plate X.

COTTAGE AT BRIMSCOMBE.

CHIMNEY AND ENTRANCE AT BRIMSCOMBE.

Plate XII.

WEST END FARM, NEAR CHIDDINGFOLD.

Plate XIII.

COMBE FARM, CHIDDINGFOLD.

Plate XIV.

THE OLD VICARAGE, CHIDDINGFOLD.

Plate XV.

AT CHIDDINGFOLD.

Plate XVI.

AT ELSTEAD.

THE 'CROWN' INN, CHIDDINGFOLD.

Plate XVII.

AT COMPTON.

Plate XVIII.

THE EAST FRONT, CROSSWAYS FARM.

THE PORCH, CROSSWAYS FARM, ABINGER HAMMER.

Plate XX.

VIEW ACROSS THE MOAT, CROWHURST PLACE.

Plate XXI.

WARREN FARMHOUSE, CROWHURST.

Plate XXII.

COTTAGES AT EASHING.

Plate XXIII.

BACK OF COTTAGES, EASHING.

Plate XXIV.

COTTAGES BY THE RIVER, EASHING.

NORTHLANDS FARM, EWHURST.

Plate XXVI.

DETAIL OF NORTHLANDS FARM, EWHURST.

Plate XXVII.

POLLINGFOLD FARMHOUSE, ELLEN'S GREEN, EWHURST.

Plate XXVIII.

AT EWHURST.

Plate XXIX.

AT EWHURST.

NEAR EASHING.

Plate XXX.

SUMMERSBURY FARMHOUSE, EWHURST.

Plate XXXI.

VIEW OF THE CHIMNEYS, THE ALMSHOUSES, FARNCOMBE.

Plate XXXII.

CHAPEL ENTRANCE TO THE ALMSHOUSES, FARNCOMBE.

COTTAGE AT HAMBLEDON.

Plate XXXIII.

STOCKHURST FARM, NEAR OXTED.

FRONT OF COTTAGES AT FARNCOMBE.

Plate XXXIV.

CASTLE STREET, FARNHAM.

Plate XXXV.

FARMHOUSE AND FOOTBRIDGE NEAR FARNHAM.

ORIEL WINDOW AT FARNHAM.

Plate XXXVI.

VIEW UP FIR GROVE HILL, FARNHAM.

DOWNING STREET, FARNHAM.

Plate XXXVII.

AT FRENSHAM.

Plate XXXVIII.

SPREAKLEY FARMHOUSE, FRENSHAM.

Plate XXXIX.

VIEW OF FROSBURY FARM.

Plate XL.

BETWEEN FROSBURY AND LITTLEFIELD FARMS.

Plate XLI.

UNSTEAD FARM, NEAR GODALMING.

UNSTEAD FARM, NEAR GODALMING.

Plate XLIII.

CHURCH ROAD, GODSTONE.

Plate XLIV.

FRONT OF HOUSES AT OOMSHALL.

Plate XLV.

COMPTON'S FARM, WOOD STREET, NEAR GUILDFORD.

Plate XLVI.

BACK OF 'STUD HOUSE,' OXTED.

COTTAGES NEAR GUILDFORD.

Plate XLVII.

SHEPHERD'S HILL, HASLEMERE.

Plate XLIX.

COTTAGES ON ROAD TO LYTHE HILL, HASLEMERE.

Plate L.

THE QUEST HOUSE, LINGFIELD.

SHOP AND COTTAGES, LINGFIELD.

Plate LIII.

AT MOUSHILL, MILFORD.

AT MOUSHILL, MILFORD.

Plate LIV.

WEST FRONT OF FARMHOUSE, MILFORD.

Plate LV.

AT SHERE.

AT NINE ELMS, MILFORD.

Plate LV.

AT SHERE.

AT NINE ELMS, MILFORD.

Plate LV.

AT SHERE.

AT NINE ELMS, MILFORD.

Plate LVI.

GROUP OF COTTAGES, HAMBLEDON.

COTTAGE AT MILFORD.

Plate LVII.

RUINED COTTAGE NEAR NORMANDY VILLAGE.

VIEW OF COTTAGE NEAR NORMANDY VILLAGE.

FARMHOUSE AND COTTAGES NEAR NORMANDY VILLAGE.

COTTAGES IN WORPLESDON VILLAGE.

MANN FARM, EAST SHALFORD, GUILDFORD.

THE 'SURREY OAKS' INN, NEAR NEWDIGATE.

Plate LXI.

BONNET'S FARM, NEAR OCKLEY.

THE PORCH, BONNET'S FARM, NEAR OCKLEY.

Plate LXIII.

SOUTH FRONT OF OSCROFT'S OR STREET'S FARM, NEAR OCKLEY.

Plate LXIV.

COTTAGE ON BANK AT PUTTENHAM.

END OF COTTAGE AT EWHURST.

Plate LXV.

THE 'ANCHOR' INN, RIPLEY.

Plate LXVI.

AT RIPLEY.

Plate LXVII.

HOLE'S COTTAGE, RIPLEY (ONCE THE MANOR HOUSE).

Plate LXVIII.

EAST END FARM, SEALE.

Plate LXIX.

EAST END FARM, SEALE.

YARD ENTRANCE, EAST END FARM, SEALE.

Plate LXXI.

THE POST OFFICE, SHAMLEY GREEN.

Plate LXXII.

BACK VIEW OF THE POST OFFICE, SHAMLEY GREEN.

Plate LXXIII.

THE POST OFFICE, SHAMLEY GREEN.

Plate LXXIV.

AT SHAMLEY GREEN.

Plate LXXV.

DETAIL VIEW OF GABLE AT SHAMLEY GREEN.

Plate LXXVI.

AT THE TOP OF SHAMLEY GREEN.

GABLED FARMHOUSE NEAR WITLEY.

Plate LXXVII.

AT SHERE.

Plate LXXVIII.

AT SHERE.

Plate LXXIX.

WOODLANDS FARM, SLYFIELD GREEN.

Plate LXXX.

NEAR SLYFIELD GREEN, GUILDFORD.

WATTS' FARM, NOW COTTAGES, NEAR SLYFIELD GREEN, GUILDFORD.

HURTMORE FARMHOUSE, NEAR GODALMING.

Plate LXXXII.

SMALLFIELD PLACE, NEAR HORLEY.

TWO VIEWS OF FARMHOUSE (NOW COTTAGES) AT STOKE, GUILDFORD.

Plate LXXXIV.

SOUTH VIEW OF COTTAGES AT STOKE, GUILDFORD.

NEAR NORMANDY VILLAGE.

Plate LXXXV.

GREAT TANGLEY MANOR.

Plate LXXXVI.

A GABLE AT GREAT TANGLEY MANOR.

Plate LXXXVII.

NEAR THURSLEY.

COTTAGE NEAR THE INN, THURSLEY.

Plate LXXXIX.

AT THURSLEY.

AT ELSTEAD.

Plate XC.

HOUSE AT GOMSHALL.

AT THURSLEY.

Plate XCI.

BARN AT TONGHAM.

CART-SHED AND GRANARY AT TONGHAM.

Plate XCIII.

TIGBOURNE FARM, NEAR WITLEY.

Plate XCIV.

THE WHITE HART INN, WITLEY.

THE VILLAGE STREET, WITLEY.
ENTRANCE TO PUTTENHAM VILLAGE.

Plate XCVI.

NEAR THE CHURCH, WITLEY.

Plate XCVII.

SLYFIELD FARM, STOKE NEAR GUILDFORD.

MANOR FARM, WITLEY.

Plate XCVIII.

HURST COTTAGES, WORPLESDON.

LITTLEFIELD FARM.

Plate XCIX.

NORTON FARMHOUSE, WORPLESDON, FRONT AND BACK VIEWS.

Plate C.

WOLVEN'S FARM, NEAR ABINGER, FRONT AND BACK VIEWS.

www.ingramcontent.com/pod-product-compliance
Lightning Source LLC
Chambersburg PA
CBHW080433110426
42743CB00016B/3152